WeightWatchers®

Recipes to serve four or more

Weekends

First published in Great Britain by Simon & Schuster UK Ltd, 2012
A CBS Company

Weight Watchers Publications: Cheryl Jackson, Jane Griffiths,
Selena Makepeace, Nina McKerlie and Imogen Prescott.

Recipes written by: Sue Ashworth, Sue Beveridge, Tamsin Burnett-Hall,
Cas Clarke, Siân Davies, Roz Denny, Nicola Graimes, Becky Johnson,
Kim Morphew, Joy Skipper, Penny Stephens and Wendy Veale as well
as Weight Watchers Leaders and Members.

Photography by: Iain Bagwell, Steve Baxter, Steve Lee, Juliet Piddington
and William Shaw.
Project editor: Nicki Lampon.
Design and typesetting: Geoff Fennell.

Colour reproduction by Dot Gradations Ltd, UK.
Printed and bound in China.

A CIP catalogue for this book is available from the British Library

ISBN 978-0-85720-936-8

1 2 3 4 5 6 7 8 9 10

Pictured on the title page: Fruit brûlée.
Pictured on the Introduction: Roast lamb with mint sauce p82, Herbed goat's cheese
pâté p52, Gourmet beef burger p68.

WeightWatchers®

Recipes to serve four or more

Weekends

SIMON &
SCHUSTER
ILLUSTRATED

London · New York · Sydney · Toronto · New Delhi

A CBS COMPANY

Weight Watchers **ProPoints** Weight Loss System is a simple way to lose weight. As part of the Weight Watchers **ProPoints** plan you'll enjoy eating delicious, healthy, filling foods that help to keep you feeling satisfied for longer and in control of your portions.

Ⓥ This symbol denotes a vegetarian recipe and assumes that, where relevant, free range eggs, vegetarian cheese, vegetarian virtually fat free fromage frais, vegetarian low fat crème fraîche and vegetarian low fat yogurts are used. Virtually fat free fromage frais, low fat crème fraîche and low fat yogurts may contain traces of gelatine so they are not always vegetarian. Please check the labels.

❄ This symbol denotes a dish that can be frozen. Unless otherwise stated, you can freeze the finished dish for up to 3 months. Defrost thoroughly and reheat until the dish is piping hot throughout.

Recipe notes

Egg size: Medium, unless otherwise stated.

Raw eggs: Only the freshest eggs should be used. Pregnant women, the elderly and children should avoid recipes with eggs that are not fully cooked or raw.

All fruits and vegetables: Medium, unless otherwise stated.

Stock: Stock cubes are used in recipes, unless otherwise stated. These should be prepared according to packet instructions.

Recipe timings: These are approximate and meant to be guidelines. Please note that the preparation time includes all the steps up to and following the main cooking time(s).

Microwaves: Timings and temperatures are for a standard 800 W microwave. If necessary, adjust your own microwave.

Low fat spread: Where a recipe states to use a low fat spread, a light spread with a fat content of no less than 38% should be used.

Low fat soft cheese: Where low fat soft cheese is specified in a recipe, this refers to soft cheese with a fat content of less than 5%.

Contents

Introduction

Weekends – a chance to spend time with family and friends and relax over leisurely meals everyone can enjoy.

Start the weekend as you mean to go on with a tempting Bacon and Egg Omelette or enjoy delicious Marmalade Muffins with friends over coffee. Have a special but light lunch with a Malaysian Chicken Salad or invite everyone round for a Sunday Pot Roast. Choose from an amazing selection of soups, starters, main meals and desserts to create a fabulous menu, or use the Party Food chapter as inspiration for entertaining.

Whatever you choose, *Weekends* is packed full of perfect sharing recipes from the best of Weight Watchers cookbooks that will make your days that bit more special.

About Weight Watchers

For more than 40 years Weight Watchers has been helping people around the world to lose weight using a long term sustainable approach. Weight Watchers successful weight loss system is based on four tried and trusted principles:

- Eating healthily
- Being more active
- Adjusting behaviour to help weight loss
- Getting support in weekly meetings

Our unique **ProPoints** system empowers you to manage your food plan and make wise recipe choices for a healthier, happier you. To find out more about Weight Watchers and the **ProPoints** values for these recipes contact Customer Services on 0845 345 1500.

Storing and freezing

Although these dishes are aimed at sharing with friends and family on the weekends, you might want to make them and store or freeze so you have leftovers for the busy week ahead. Many dishes store well in the fridge, but make sure you use them up within a day or two. Some can also be frozen. However, it is important to make sure you know how to freeze safely.

- Wrap any food to be frozen in rigid containers or strong freezer bags. This is important to stop foods contaminating each other or getting freezer burn.
- Label the containers or bags with the contents and date – your freezer should have a star marking that tells you how long you can keep different types of frozen food.
- Never freeze warm food – always let it cool completely first.
- Never freeze food that has already been frozen and defrosted.
- Freeze food in portions, then you can take out as little or as much as you need each time.
- Defrost what you need in the fridge, making sure you put anything that might have juices, such as meat, on a covered plate or in a container.
- Fresh food, such as raw meat and fish, should be wrapped and frozen as soon as possible.
- Most fruit and vegetables can be frozen by open freezing. Lay them out on a tray, freeze until solid and then pack them into bags.
- Some vegetables, such as peas, broccoli and broad beans can be blanched first by cooking for 2 minutes in boiling water. Drain, refresh under cold water and then freeze once cold.
- Fresh herbs are great frozen – either seal leaves in bags or, for soft herbs such as basil and parsley, chop finely and add to ice cube trays with water. These are great for dropping into casseroles or soups straight from the freezer.

Some things cannot be frozen. Whole eggs do not freeze well, but yolks and whites can be frozen separately. Vegetables with a high water content, such as salad leaves, celery and cucumber, will not freeze. Fried foods will be soggy if frozen, and sauces such as mayonnaise will separate when thawed and should not be frozen.

Shopping hints and tips

Always buy the best ingredients you can afford. If you are going to cook healthy meals, it is worth investing in some quality ingredients that will really add flavour to your dishes. When buying meat, choose lean cuts of meat or lean mince, and if you are buying prepacked cooked sliced meat, buy it fresh from the deli counter. Packaged cooked meat usually has salt and preservatives added.

For dressings, choose the best quality balsamic vinegar you can afford and a good quality olive oil. Try a few brands to find the one you like.

When you're going around the supermarket it's tempting to pick up foods you like and put them in your trolley without thinking about how you will use them. So, a good plan is to decide what dishes you want to cook before you go shopping, check your store cupboard and make a list of what you need. You'll save time by not drifting aimlessly around the supermarket picking up what you fancy.

We've added a checklist here for some of the store cupboard ingredients used in this book. Just add fresh ingredients in your regular shop and you'll be ready to cook the delicious recipes in *Weekends*.

Store cupboard checklist

- [ ] allspice
- [ ] anchovies, canned
- [ ] apricots, dried ready to eat
- [ ] artificial sweetener
- [ ] baked beans, canned
- [ ] baking powder
- [ ] bay leaves
- [ ] bicarbonate of soda
- [ ] bouquet garni
- [ ] bulgar wheat, dried
- [ ] butter beans, canned
- [ ] capers
- [ ] cayenne pepper
- [ ] chick peas, canned
- [ ] chilli (flakes and powder)
- [ ] Chinese five spice
- [ ] chocolate (70% cocoa solids)
- [ ] cinnamon sticks
- [ ] cinnamon, ground
- [ ] cloves
- [ ] cocoa powder
- [ ] coconut, dessicated
- [ ] cooking spray, calorie controlled
- [ ] coriander seeds

- [ ] coriander, ground
- [ ] cornflour
- [ ] couscous, dried
- [ ] crab meat, canned in brine
- [ ] cumin seeds
- [ ] cumin, ground
- [ ] currants
- [ ] curry powder
- [ ] flour (plain and self raising)
- [ ] garam masala
- [ ] ginger, ground
- [ ] golden syrup
- [ ] herbs, dried (mixed and Italian)
- [ ] honey, runny
- [ ] jam, reduced sugar
- [ ] lasagne sheets, dried
- [ ] lime leaves, dried
- [ ] mango chutney
- [ ] mixed spice
- [ ] mushrooms, dried
- [ ] mustard (Dijon and wholegrain)
- [ ] noodles, dried
- [ ] oil (vegetable and olive)
- [ ] olives in brine, black

- [ ] passata
- [ ] pasta, dried
- [ ] paprika
- [ ] peppercorns
- [ ] pesto sauce
- [ ] pimientos, canned
- [ ] pizza dough mix
- [ ] prunes, canned in natural juice
- [ ] raisins
- [ ] rice, dried basmati
- [ ] saffron
- [ ] salt
- [ ] sesame seeds
- [ ] soy sauce
- [ ] stock cubes
- [ ] sugar (caster and soft brown)
- [ ] sultanas
- [ ] tomato purée
- [ ] tomatoes, canned
- [ ] turmeric
- [ ] vanilla extract
- [ ] vinegar (balsamic and white wine)
- [ ] Worcestershire sauce

Brunches and lunches

Bacon and potato omelette

Serves 6
156 calories per serving
Takes 20 minutes + cooling
❄

calorie controlled cooking spray
1 onion, sliced thinly
4 x 25 g (1 oz) lean back bacon rashers, cut into short strips
6 eggs
2 tablespoons chopped fresh parsley
350 g (12 oz) leftover cooked potatoes, sliced
salt and freshly ground black pepper

This can be served cold for breakfast on the run (or a picnic lunch) or hot with baked beans as part of a brunch.

1 Heat a non stick frying pan, about 25 cm (10 inches) in diameter, and spray with the cooking spray. Gently sauté the onion for a couple of minutes and then add the bacon and cook for another 2 minutes.

2 Meanwhile, beat the eggs in a large bowl with the parsley and plenty of seasoning. Add the cooked onion and bacon and the potatoes to the eggs and stir well.

3 Respray the pan and heat over a medium heat. Pour the egg mixture into the pan. Check that everything is evenly distributed, turn the heat down and leave to cook gently for 5 minutes while you preheat the grill to medium.

4 Put the pan under the grill for 5 minutes or until the eggs are completely set and the top is golden. Leave to cool in the pan for 10 minutes.

5 Remove the omelette by easing the edges with a palette knife or spatula and flipping it on to a plate. Cut into six slices to serve.

Tip... If you prefer not to use the grill, you can carefully invert the frittata on to a plate after the initial cooking and then slide it back into the pan to cook for 5 minutes on the other side.

Smoky fish patties

Serves 4

208 calories per serving

Takes 20 minutes to prepare,
  15–20 minutes to cook

❄

600 g (1 lb 5 oz) potatoes,
  peeled and chopped

350 g (12 oz) smoked haddock
  fillets, skinned

1 bay leaf

8 spring onions, chopped
  finely

4 tablespoons finely chopped
  fresh parsley

calorie controlled cooking
  spray

freshly ground black pepper

*These delicious patties are easy to make and can be
served with a green salad for lunch or on their own for
a great brunch.*

1 Bring a large saucepan of water to the boil, add the potatoes
and simmer for 15–20 minutes until tender. Drain them well
and mash.

2 Meanwhile, place the haddock in a wide, shallow, lidded,
non stick frying pan and pour over enough water to just cover.
Add the bay leaf, bring to the boil, reduce the heat, cover and
simmer for 5 minutes until the fish flakes. Drain the fish, remove
the bay leaf and leave to cool slightly.

3 Flake the haddock and add to the mash with the spring onions
and parsley. Season with freshly ground black pepper (the fish
will probably make the mixture salty enough).

4 Shape the mixture into eight patties. Spray a non stick frying
pan with the cooking spray and heat until hot. Add the patties
and fry for 5 minutes, turning once, until golden and hot in the
middle. You may need to do this in batches. Serve two patties
each.

Tip... To freeze, shape into patties and open freeze before
wrapping in cling film and packing into a freezerproof
container.

Mushroom sloppy joes

Serves 4

151 calories per serving

Takes 10 minutes to prepare, 15 minutes to cook

Sloppy Joes are a popular American dish, normally made with mince. This mushroom version is simply delicious.

1 Place the mushrooms and garlic in a non stick saucepan, spray with the cooking spray and cook them gently for 5 minutes.

2 Add the stock, season and cook over a high heat for 5 minutes. Stir in the soup and heat through.

3 Add the crème fraîche and stir well. Remove from the heat. Toast the bread.

4 Top the four slices of toast with the mixture. Scatter over the parsley and serve.

Variation... There is such a wide variety of mushrooms available in supermarkets. Try experimenting with different types such as oyster, shiitake or brown cap mushrooms.

350 g (12 oz) large button mushrooms, quartered

2 garlic cloves, crushed

calorie controlled cooking spray

150 ml (5 fl oz) vegetable stock

290 g can low fat condensed mushroom soup

2 tablespoons half fat crème fraîche

4 medium slices wholemeal bread

salt and freshly ground black pepper

1 tablespoon chopped fresh parsley, to garnish

Breakfast pancakes

Makes 12 pancakes
47 calories per serving
Takes 10 minutes to prepare,
  15 minutes to cook
Ⓥ

75 g (2¾ oz) plain flour
25 g (1 oz) wholemeal flour
½ teaspoon baking powder
1 egg
1 tablespoon clear honey
300 ml (10 fl oz) skimmed milk
calorie controlled cooking
  spray

These are especially nice served for a leisurely breakfast or brunch.

1 Put the flours, baking powder, egg, honey and skimmed milk in a large bowl and beat well until smooth.

2 Spray a heavy based non stick frying pan with the cooking spray and heat. When the pan is hot, drop in heaped tablespoons of the pancake mixture, 3–4 at a time, and cook until the top almost sets and bubbles start to rise.

3 Flip the pancakes over and cook the other side briefly. Repeat the cooking process with the remaining batter.

Variation... For a more filling brunch, add 3 tablespoons of cooked brown rice to the batter.

Eggs benedict rolls

Serves 4
166 calories per serving
Takes 20 minutes

4 eggs
¼ teaspoon artificial sweetener
1 tablespoon white wine vinegar
25 g (1 oz) Quark
juice of ½ a small lemon
1 tablespoon finely chopped fresh tarragon
100 ml (3½ fl oz) skimmed milk
calorie controlled cooking spray
2 large tomatoes, sliced thinly
8 x 15 g (½ oz) Parma ham slices
30 g (1¼ oz) baby spinach leaves, washed
salt and freshly ground black pepper

This is a really satisfying breakfast treat.

1 Put 2.5 cm (1 inch) of cold water in a saucepan and bring to the boil. Meanwhile, separate two of the eggs, put the egg yolks in a medium heatproof bowl (one that fits snugly over the saucepan) and reserve the egg whites in a jug.

2 To make the sauce, lower the heat in the saucepan to barely a simmer. Add the sweetener and vinegar to the egg yolks and place the bowl over the pan of simmering water. Using an electric whisk, whisk the egg yolks for 3–5 minutes until they are three times the original volume and very thick. Remove from the heat, season and stir in the Quark, lemon juice and tarragon. Set aside.

3 Add the remaining eggs and milk to the reserved egg whites, season and whisk gently. Heat a non stick frying pan, spray with the cooking spray and pour in a quarter of the beaten egg. Swirl the pan quickly to spread the beaten egg and make a thin pancake. Cook for 1–2 minutes until golden underneath and set on the top. Transfer to a warm plate and keep warm. Repeat to make three more egg pancakes, putting non stick baking parchment between each pancake on the warm plate.

4 To serve, spread each pancake with a little of the sauce and scatter with the tomato slices, two slices of Parma ham and baby spinach leaves. Roll up like a wrap, cut in half and serve immediately.

 Variation... You can use a 100 g packet of Quorn Deli Ham Style Slices, in place of the Parma ham.

Sweet French toast

Serves 4
124 calories per serving
Takes 15 minutes
Ⓥ

2 small eggs, beaten
100 ml (3½ fl oz) skimmed milk
12 x 1 cm (½ inch) slices French stick
calorie controlled cooking spray
1 tablespoon artificial sweetener, to serve

Everyone loves French toast – perfect for a special brunch.

1 In a large mixing bowl, mix together the eggs and milk.

2 Add the slices of bread to the bowl. Turn over a few times to make sure they are thoroughly coated with the egg mixture. Leave to soak for a couple of minutes so that they can absorb the egg.

3 Meanwhile, spray a large non stick frying pan with the cooking spray and warm to a medium heat. Fry the slices of bread in batches for 1–2 minutes on each side or until golden brown. Keep the cooked French toast warm in the oven until everything is ready. Sprinkle with the sweetener and serve three slices each.

Variation... If you don't have a sweet tooth, try making cheese and ham French toast. Cut the French stick into 6 x 2.5 cm (1 inch) slices and then make a pocket in each slice by carefully cutting into it along one side. Fill the pockets with 50 g (1¾ oz) of half fat grated Cheddar cheese and 30 g (1¼ oz) of wafer thin ham, finely chopped. Use as in the above recipe, seasoning the egg mix and omitting the sweetener.

Crunchy nectarine yogurt pots

Serves 4
237 calories per serving
Takes 10 minutes + cooling
Ⓨ

4 ripe nectarines or peaches,
stoned and quartered
2 pieces pared lemon rind
4 tablespoons honey
300 g (10½ oz) 0% fat Greek
yogurt
80 g (3 oz) granola

This is a healthy start to the day or could be served as a
refreshing dessert at the end of a meal.

1 Place the nectarines or peaches in a small lidded pan with
the lemon rind and pour over 200 ml (7 fl oz) of water. Bring to
the boil, cover and simmer for 5 minutes until the fruit is just
soft. Drizzle over the honey and set aside to cool completely.

2 Take four serving glasses, place two pieces of fruit in the
base of each and cover with 2 heaped tablespoons of the
yogurt and then ½ tablespoon of granola. Repeat, ending with
the granola.

Tip... Poached fruit will keep covered in the fridge for up
to 3 days.

Variation... You could try this with eight small or four large
plums, instead of the nectarines, as an alternative.

Marmalade muffins

Makes 10 muffins
94 calories per serving
Takes 35 minutes
Ⓥ
❄ (reheat to serve)

150 g (5½ oz) self raising flour
¼ teaspoon baking powder
**2 tablespoons artificial
sweetener**
1 egg, beaten
**50 g (1¾ oz) low fat natural
yogurt**
juice of ½ a large orange
**5 tablespoons reduced sugar
orange jam or marmalade**
**50 g (1¾ oz) low fat spread,
melted**

These muffins are delicious for brunch, afternoon tea or in lunch boxes.

1 Preheat the oven to Gas Mark 5/190°C/fan oven 170°C. Place 10 paper cases in a muffin tin.

2 Mix the flour, baking powder and sweetener together in a large bowl. Beat the egg, yogurt, orange juice, jam or marmalade and melted low fat spread together in a smaller bowl.

3 Gently stir the wet ingredients into the dry (see Tip) and then quickly spoon into the muffin cases. Bake for 25 minutes or until the muffins are well risen and golden on top.

4 Remove from the oven and allow to cool in the tin for 5 minutes before transferring to a wire rack.

Tip... It's best to use a very light and quick hand to mix muffins – stop after a maximum of ten stirs. Lumps in the mixture do not matter, in fact they signify the lightness to come.

paragus, spring onion and bacon hash

Serves 4

178 calories per serving

Takes 15 minutes to prepare,
35 minutes to cook

**450 g (1 lb) new potatoes,
scrubbed**

**4 x 25 g (1 oz) lean back
bacon rashers**

100 g (3½ oz) fine asparagus

6 spring onions, sliced

1 tablespoon olive oil

**1 teaspoon wholegrain
mustard**

**salt and freshly ground black
pepper**

*Real comfort food. Be sure not to over-mash the potatoes;
this dish should have a chunky texture. Serve with
2 tablespoons of tomato ketchup per person if you wish.*

1 Bring a saucepan of water to the boil, add the new potatoes
and simmer for 20 minutes until cooked through. Drain well
and crush roughly with a potato masher.

2 Meanwhile, preheat the grill to medium-high and grill the
bacon until crispy. Snip into small pieces.

3 Bring another saucepan of water to the boil, add the
asparagus and cook for 2 minutes. Drain thoroughly and toss
with the snipped bacon, spring onions and crushed potatoes
to make the hash.

4 Heat the olive oil and mustard in a large non stick frying pan,
add the hash mixture and stir fry for 10 minutes over a medium
heat, turning with a wooden spatula from time to time. Season
to taste and serve hot.

Tip... Mix 1 tablespoonful of tomato purée with 1 skinned,
de-seeded and diced fresh tomato and seasoning.

Malaysian chicken salad

Serves 4
173 calories per serving
Takes 15 minutes

330 g (11½ oz) cooked skinless boneless chicken breasts, shredded

2 large carrots, peeled and sliced into thin matchsticks

½ large cucumber, sliced into thin matchsticks

6 spring onions, shredded

1 red pepper, de-seeded and sliced into thin matchsticks

200 g (7 oz) beansprouts

85 g (3 oz) watercress, chopped roughly

a small bunch of fresh mint or coriander, chopped roughly

For the dressing

juice of 2 limes

1 tablespoon light soy sauce

2 teaspoons sesame oil

It speeds things up to shred all the vegetables in a food processor or with a vegetable mandolin if you have one; otherwise chop them by hand with a very sharp knife.

1 Combine all the salad ingredients in a bowl.

2 Either shake the dressing ingredients together in a screw top jar or whisk them together in a bowl. Pour over the salad, toss together and serve.

Tip... Shred the chicken breast by hand – just pull it apart along the grain of the meat.

Smoky beef

Serves 6
170 calories per serving
Takes 30 minutes

juice of 2 limes
1 teaspoon smoked paprika
½ teaspoon mixed spice
1 teaspoon garam masala
250 g packet fresh cooked beetroot in natural juice, drained and cut into wedges
2 red peppers, de-seeded and cut into large pieces
½ teaspoon cumin seeds, crushed lightly
calorie controlled cooking spray
600 g (1 lb 5 oz) lean beef fillet, visible fat removed and cut in half lengthways
½ x 25 g packet fresh coriander, chopped roughly

Serve with 100 g (3½ oz) of new potatoes per person.

1 Preheat the oven to Gas Mark 7/220°C/fan oven 200°C and put a non stick baking tray in to heat. Mix together the lime juice, paprika, mixed spice and garam masala to make a paste. Set aside.

2 Remove the tray from the oven and scatter over the beetroot, peppers and cumin seeds. Spray with the cooking spray and return the tray to the oven.

3 Heat a wide non stick frying pan until hot and spray both beef fillets with the cooking spray. Cook the fillets together for 3–4 minutes until brown all over. Transfer to a board and brush over the top and sides with the spice paste.

4 Remove the tray from the oven, make a space in the middle of the vegetables and transfer the fillets to this space. Roast in the oven for 15 minutes until the vegetables are lightly charred.

5 Remove the tray from the oven again and transfer the fillets to a carving board. Loosely cover with foil. Stir the coriander through the vegetables. Carve the fillets into thin slices. Serve with the vegetables.

Piadina

Serves 4

220 calories per serving

Takes 15 minutes

Ⓥ

1 small aubergine, sliced into rounds

1 small courgette, sliced thinly lengthways

3 canned artichoke hearts, drained and halved

calorie controlled cooking spray

2 plum tomatoes, sliced

75 g (2¾ oz) light mozzarella cheese, drained and sliced

4 x 50 g (1¾ oz) multigrain tortilla wraps (about 20 cm/ 8 inches in diameter)

a handful of fresh basil leaves

salt and freshly ground black pepper

Piadina ia a thin Italian flatbread. Here we use tortilla wraps for speed but the result is just as delicious.

1 Heat a ridged griddle pan or non stick frying pan until hot. Spray the aubergine, courgette and artichokes with the cooking spray and cook them in batches, turning once until charred and softened. Keep warm while you cook all the batches.

2 Arrange the vegetables, tomatoes and mozzarella between two of the wraps. Scatter over the basil and season. Top with the other two wraps, press down and spray the top with the cooking spray. Carefully turn over, placing the sprayed side on the griddle or frying pan.

3 Cook for 1 minute. Spray the top with the cooking spray. Using a wide spatula, turn it over. Cook for 1 minute. Remove from the pan and keep warm while you cook the other piadina. Cut into quarters and serve two quarters each.

Courgette and pesto pasta with halloumi

Serves 4

381 calories per serving

Takes 30 minutes

Ⓥ

240 g (8½ oz) dried conchiglie pasta

2 courgettes, cut into ribbons (see Tip)

calorie controlled cooking spray

175 g (6 oz) halloumi, cut into thin slices

3 tablespoons reduced fat pesto

a handful of fresh basil leaves, to garnish

This is a lovely summer pasta dish that uses the Greek cheese halloumi.

1 Bring a large saucepan of water to the boil, add the pasta and cook according to the packet instructions. Drain, reserving 4 tablespoons of cooking liquid.

2 Meanwhile, heat a griddle pan or non stick frying pan until hot. Spray the courgette ribbons with the cooking spray and cook for 1–2 minutes, turning once, until charred and just cooked. You may have to do this in batches.

3 Spray the halloumi slices with the cooking spray and cook in the griddle or frying pan for 2–3 minutes, turning once, until golden.

4 Return the pasta to the saucepan with the reserved cooking liquid, courgette ribbons and the pesto. Stir to combine and heat gently for 2–3 minutes until hot. Serve the pasta in large bowls topped with the halloumi and some basil leaves to garnish.

Tip... Use a vegetable peeler to cut the ribbons of courgette.

Greek chicken in pitta

Serves 4
349 calories per serving
Takes 20 minutes
❄ (chicken and unfilled
    pittas only)

2 tablespoons lime juice
1 teaspoon coriander seeds,
    crushed
1 teaspoon ground cumin
2 tablespoons chopped fresh
    mint leaves
250 g (9 oz) skinless mini
    chicken fillets
100 g (3½ oz) reduced fat
    houmous
100 g (3½ oz) 0% fat Greek
    yogurt
¼ Iceberg lettuce, shredded
½ red onion, cut into rings
1 red pepper, de-seeded and
    sliced
4 tomatoes, quartered
½ cucumber, diced
20 black olives, stoned
8 mini pitta breads

Want to feel as if you're on a sunny beach? You may not get the weather, but this recipe should bring you all the right flavours.

1 In a bowl, mix the lime juice with the coriander seeds, cumin and a tablespoon of the mint leaves. Roll the chicken fillets in this to coat them and put on one side until ready to cook.

2 Mix together the houmous and yogurt. Preheat the grill to medium-high.

3 Meanwhile, arrange the lettuce, onion, pepper, tomatoes, cucumber and olives on a plate or in a bowl. Sprinkle with the remaining chopped mint.

4 Grill the chicken for 5 minutes on each side or until the meat is cooked through. A few minutes before the end of the cooking time, put the mini pittas under the grill and toast on each side for a minute or two. Alternatively, you can toast the pittas in a toaster.

5 Cut the chicken fillets in half lengthways and open the pittas by splitting them halfway round the edge. Fill the pittas with the chicken fillets and half of the houmous mix. Serve accompanied by the salad and the remaining houmous mix.

Variations... If you're in a hurry, you could substitute 250 g (9 oz) of ready roasted skinless chicken fillets, cut into strips, for the marinated chicken.

oasted rosemary vegetables on ciabatta

Serves 4

425 calories per serving

Takes 10 minutes to prepare,
25 minutes to cook

Ⓥ

❄

1 red pepper, de-seeded and
  roughly diced

1 green pepper, de-seeded and
  roughly diced

1 courgette, thickly sliced

175 g (6 oz) open cap
  mushrooms, halved

1 tablespoon olive oil

1 teaspoon balsamic vinegar

2 fresh rosemary sprigs

2 whole garlic cloves

4 tomatoes, quartered

1 ciabatta loaf, halved
  horizontally

2 tablespoons sun-dried
  tomato purée

salt and freshly ground black
  pepper

*This is a bit like a posh pizza and is delicious served warm
or cold. Wrap well in plenty of greaseproof paper and foil
for an excellent lunchtime snack.*

1 Preheat the oven to Gas Mark 6/200°C/fan oven 180°C.
Place the peppers, courgette and mushrooms in a bowl. Add
the oil and vinegar, season and toss together well.

2 Arrange on a baking tray and add the rosemary and garlic
cloves. Roast in the oven for 20 minutes. Add the tomato
quarters and return to the oven for 5 minutes.

3 Cut each ciabatta half in half again and spread with the
sun-dried tomato purée. Warm through in the oven for
5 minutes.

4 To serve, pile the roasted vegetables on to the ciabatta,
discarding the rosemary and whole garlic cloves. Serve hot.

Variation... You can use almost any vegetable you prefer as
a topping. Next time, try adding baby corn, wedges of red
onion, aubergine or celery.

Prawn, crab and baby new potato salad

Serves 4

292 calories per serving

Takes 15 minutes to prepare
+ 10 minutes cooling,
20 minutes to cook

750 g (1 lb 10 oz) baby new
  potatoes, scrubbed

2 tablespoons sun-dried
  tomato paste

2 tablespoons lime or lemon
  juice

6 spring onions, finely
  chopped

175 g (6 oz) cherry tomatoes,
  halved

125 g (4½ oz) canned red
  pimientos, drained and
  sliced

170 g can crab meat in brine,
  drained

225 g (8 oz) large, cooked,
  peeled prawns, defrosted if
  frozen

1 tablespoon capers

a few fresh basil leaves

salt and freshly ground black
  pepper

lime or lemon wedges, to serve

Make the most of new potatoes by including them in wonderful salads like this one.

1 Bring a saucepan of water to the boil, add the potatoes and simmer gently until just tender, about 15–20 minutes.

2 Meanwhile, in a serving bowl, mix together the sun-dried tomato paste with the lime or lemon juice.

3 Drain the cooked potatoes and add to the bowl, tossing them in the dressing. Allow them to cool for about 10 minutes.

4 When the potatoes have cooled, add the spring onions, tomatoes, pimientos and crab meat, stirring gently to mix. Season, pile on to serving plates and top with the prawns.

5 Sprinkle the salads with the capers and basil leaves and serve with the lime or lemon wedges to squeeze over.

Tip... Coating the hot potatoes with the dressing means that they will absorb more of its flavour.

Lamb koftas

Makes 10

179 calories per serving

Takes 15 minutes to prepare + 20 minutes chilling + soaking, 12–15 minutes to cook

For the koftas

500 g (1 lb 2 oz) lamb mince

1 egg yolk

100 g (3½ oz) fresh white breadcrumbs

1 onion, chopped

1 tablespoon chopped fresh parsley

½ teaspoon ground cinnamon

1 teaspoon ground cumin

½ teaspoon chilli powder

1 teaspoon turmeric

½ teaspoon ground allspice

For the sauce

150 g (5½ oz) low fat natural yogurt

juice of ½ a lemon

1 tablespoon tahini paste

2 garlic cloves, crushed

A great recipe for a summer lunch – skewers of spicy lamb that can be cooked on the barbecue and served with a crunchy salad.

1 Soak 10 wooden kebab skewers in water for at least 30 minutes.

2 Place all the kofta ingredients in a food processor and blend until completely mixed.

3 Using wet hands, form the mixture into balls and squeeze on to the end of the skewers. Place on a plate or tray and cover with cling film. Leave to chill in the fridge for 20 minutes.

4 In a bowl, mix together the sauce ingredients and place in the fridge until ready to serve.

5 Heat the grill until hot and cook the koftas for about 12–15 minutes, turning quite often to prevent them from burning. If using a barbecue the same applies – keep checking them to prevent burning.

6 Serve with the tahini and yogurt sauce.

Tip... Soaking the kebab skewers prevents them from burning when the koftas are cooking.

Salmon Niçoise salad

Serves 4
234 calories per serving
Takes 15 minutes to prepare,
20 minutes to cook

**200 g (7 oz) baby new
potatoes, scrubbed**

**300 g (10½ oz) green beans,
trimmed**

**2 x 150 g (5½ oz) salmon
fillets**

**4 Little Gem lettuces or Cos
lettuce hearts, shredded**

**250 g (9 oz) cherry tomatoes,
halved**

**8 black olives, stoned and
chopped**

1 red onion, sliced finely

a bunch of fresh basil, torn

**salt and freshly ground black
pepper**

For the dressing

**grated zest and juice of a
lemon**

**1 teaspoon dried oregano or
herbes de Provence**

1 tablespoon Dijon mustard

*Fresh salmon is delicious and pretty in this classic
summer salad.*

1 Bring a large lidded saucepan of water to the boil, add the
new potatoes and cook for 15 minutes until they are tender.
About 5 minutes before the end of the cooking time, put the
green beans on top of the boiling potatoes and cover the pan
to steam the beans. Drain the beans and potatoes together
and refresh under cold water.

2 Meanwhile, preheat the grill to medium and place the salmon
fillets, skin side down, on a foil lined grill pan. Season and grill
for 8–10 minutes, until just cooked through and crispy golden
on top. Take off the foil, leaving the skin behind, and flake the
fish into large pieces.

3 Use the lettuce leaves to line four plates or serving bowls.
Place the potatoes, beans, tomatoes, olives, onion and basil in
a bowl. Mix together the dressing ingredients and add to the
bowl. Mix well and season.

4 Pile the dressed salad on top of the lettuce and then scatter
with the salmon pieces. Serve.

Latino chicken drummers

Serves 4
300 calories per serving
Takes 27 minutes
❄ (chicken only)

2 teaspoons ground coriander

100 g (3½ oz) mild piquante peppers, drained and chopped finely

grated zest of a lime

4 tablespoons low fat natural yogurt

750 g (1 lb 10 oz) chicken drumsticks, skin removed

250 g (9 oz) passata

a generous pinch of cayenne pepper

2 teaspoons artificial sweetener

a few dashes of Worcestershire sauce

Serve with a mixed salad and a 225 g (8 oz) potato, baked in its skin, per person.

1 Preheat the oven to Gas Mark 6/200°C/fan oven180°C and put a baking tray in to heat.

2 Put the coriander, peppers and lime zest into a food processor and whizz until finely chopped. Gradually add the yogurt, whizzing after each addition until a coarse paste forms.

3 Score three cuts into each chicken drumstick and put into a large freezer bag. Add the yogurt mixture and massage the marinade into the drumsticks.

4 Remove the baking tray from the oven, transfer the chicken to the tray and bake for 20 minutes until cooked and the juices run clear.

5 Meanwhile, put the passata, cayenne pepper, sweetener and Worcestershire sauce into a small saucepan. Bring to the boil, reduce the heat and let it bubble for 5–8 minutes until really thick, stirring occasionally. Serve the chicken drumsticks with the spicy ketchup on the side.

Soups and starters

Springtime soup

Serves 4

116 calories per serving

Takes 15 minutes to prepare,
20 minutes to cook

Ⓥ

❄

calorie controlled cooking
    spray

2 leeks, chopped finely

2 celery sticks, diced finely

400 g can chopped tomatoes

450 g (1 lb) courgettes, diced
    finely

4 carrots, peeled and diced
    finely

200 g (7 oz) green beans,
    trimmed and sliced finely

1 teaspoon dried
    Mediterranean herbs

1.2 litres (2 pints) vegetable
    stock

a bunch of fresh flat leaf
    parsley or basil, chopped

salt and freshly ground black
    pepper

50 g (1¾ oz) low fat soft
    cheese with garlic and
    herbs, to serve

*A simple and satisfying soup, filled with wonderful fresh
vegetables and made luxurious by the soft cheese.
Guaranteed to hit the spot everytime.*

1 Spray a large non stick saucepan with the cooking spray,
add the leeks and celery and cook for 5 minutes, adding a
splash of water if they start to stick

2 Add the tomatoes, all the other vegetables and the dried
herbs. Mix everything together and then pour over the stock.
Bring to the boil and simmer for 10 minutes.

3 Season and add the parsley or basil. Serve in warmed bowls
topped with a teaspoon of the soft cheese and a grinding of
black pepper.

Mussel broth with croûtes

Serves 4

160 calories per serving

Takes 20 minutes to prepare,
  20 minutes to cook

**1 kg (2 lb 4 oz) mussels
  (weight with shells)**
850 ml (1½ pints) fish stock
1 garlic clove, sliced
2 shallots, sliced thinly
**2 tomatoes, de-seeded and
  diced**
**2 tablespoons chopped fresh
  tarragon**

For the croûtes

1 garlic clove
**8 x 15 g (½ oz) slices French
  stick**
**calorie controlled cooking
  spray**

Ideal for summer eating.

1 To clean the mussels, scrub off any dirt and remove any barnacles. Remove the beard, if any, that sticks out between the shells. Discard any that are already open or have a cracked shell.

2 In a large lidded saucepan, bring the stock to the boil. Add the garlic and shallots and simmer for 5 minutes. Add the mussels, cover and reduce the heat. Cook for 2–3 minutes until most of the shells have opened. Discard any that don't open.

3 Use a slotted spoon to remove the mussels. Remove the mussels from all but eight of the shells. Set aside the eight. Place the mussels and stock in a food processor, or use a hand held blender, and blend until smooth. Return to the pan with the tomatoes, tarragon and reserved shelled mussels. Heat gently to warm through.

4 To make the croûtes, preheat the oven to Gas Mark 6/200°C/fan oven 180°C. Cut the garlic clove in half and rub the cut side over the bread. Spray with the cooking spray and place on a baking tray. Bake for 10–12 minutes until golden.

5 Serve the soup in warmed bowls garnished with two mussels each and two croûtes on the side.

Curried parsnip soup

Serves 4

195 calories per serving

Takes 10 minutes to prepare,
 40 minutes to cook

Ⓥ

calorie controlled cooking
 spray

1 large onion, chopped

1 garlic clove, chopped

½ red or green chilli,
 de-seeded and chopped
 finely (optional)

900 g (2 lbs) parsnips, peeled
 and chopped roughly

2 teaspoons ground coriander

1 teaspoon turmeric

1 teaspoon ground ginger

1.2 litres (2 pints) vegetable or
 chicken stock

salt and freshly ground black
 pepper

A classic recipe for a thick parsnip soup with a mild curry flavour and optional chilli depending on whether you like your food spicy.

1 Heat a large, lidded, non stick saucepan and spray with the cooking spray. Add the onion, garlic and chilli and cook for about 5 minutes until soft, adding a splash of water if they start to stick.

2 Add the parsnips and spices, cover and cook very gently for 20 minutes, stirring occasionally, until the parsnips are really soft.

3 Add the stock and season. Bring to the boil and simmer for a further 10 minutes. Using a blender, or a hand held blender, whizz until smooth. Return to the pan to reheat through if necessary, check the seasoning and serve.

Herbed goat's cheese pâté

Serves 4

155 calories per serving

Takes 5 minutes to prepare
  + 1 hour chilling

Ⓨ

150 g (5½ oz) medium fat
  French soft goat's cheese

1 tablespoon finely chopped
  fresh parsley

½ tablespoon finely chopped
  fresh dill

½ teaspoon garlic purée

3 tablespoons low fat fromage
  frais

zest of ½ a lemon

15 g (½ oz) small capers in
  sherry vinegar, drained

50 g (1¾ oz) half fat mature
  Cheddar cheese, grated

freshly ground black pepper

2 tablespoons snipped fresh
  chives, to garnish

This makes a great dinner party starter, spooned into small ramekins to make individual portions. Serve with chicory leaves and six melba toast per person.

1 In a bowl, mix together the goat's cheese, parsley, dill, garlic purée, fromage frais, lemon zest, capers and Cheddar cheese until combined. Season with freshly ground black pepper and spoon into a 300 ml (10 fl oz) dish. Sprinkle over the chives and gently press down with the back of a spoon.

2 Chill for 1 hour and serve when needed.

Tip... This will last for up to 3 days, covered in the fridge.

Capri salad

Serves 4

102 calories per serving

Takes 15 minutes

Ⓥ

4 beefsteak tomatoes

50 g (1¾ oz) stoned black or green olives in brine, drained and sliced

2 tablespoons capers in brine, rinsed

12 fresh basil leaves, plus extra to garnish

125 g packet mozzarella light, drained, cut into 8 slices and each slice halved

salt and freshly ground black pepper

2 tablespoons balsamic vinegar, to serve

This warm tomato and mozzarella stack is easy to assemble and makes an impressive supper party starter.

1 Preheat the grill to medium. Cut thin slices from the top and bottom of each tomato and discard and then slice each tomato horizontally into four slices.

2 Line a grill pan with foil. Place a slice of tomato on the foil, scatter over a few olive slices, a few capers and a basil leaf and season. Finish with a slice of mozzarella. Repeat the layers described above and make four stacks in total, starting with a tomato slice and ending with a slice of mozzarella on the top. Grill for 2–5 minutes until warm and the cheese has begun to melt.

3 Serve each stack drizzled with ½ a tablespoon of balsamic vinegar and garnished with the basil leaves.

Variations... If you prefer, you can simply arrange the ingredients on a plate instead of making stacks, and enjoy it as a cold salad.

Fresh oregano or thyme, together or separately, work well as alternatives to the basil.

Warm balsamic pears with bacon

Serves 4
97 calories per serving
Takes 20 minutes

4 whole pears, peeled and
  cored
3 tablespoons balsamic
  vinegar
1 teaspoon artificial sweetener
1 star anise
1 piece pared lemon rind
2 x 25 g (1 oz) lean back
  bacon rashers
a handful of rocket, to serve

*This makes a great dinner party starter, or serve two pears
and a rasher of bacon per person with a large salad for a
lunch for two.*

1 Lay the pears in a lidded saucepan so that they fit snugly.
Mix together the balsamic vinegar and sweetener with
150 ml (5 fl oz) of water and pour over the pears. Add the
star anise and lemon rind, cover and bring slowly to a simmer.
Cook for 10 minutes until the pears are just tender. You may
need to turn them so that they get an even colour. When
cooked, remove from the heat, carefully take out the pears
and set aside. Bring the juice back to the boil and simmer
uncovered for 2–3 minutes to reduce.

2 Meanwhile, preheat the grill to high and cook the bacon
until crispy. Cut into small strips.

3 To serve, slice the pears, place on a plate, drizzle over the
juices and scatter with the bacon. Garnish with rocket.

Variation... For an interesting dessert, omit the bacon
and rocket, cool the pears, cover and chill. Serve with a
60 g (2 oz) scoop of low fat ice cream and the juice
drizzled over.

Garlic prawn and beansprout pancakes

Serves 4

164 calories per serving

Takes 20 minutes to prepare,
  15 minutes to cook

❄

1 teaspoon sesame oil

1 teaspoon Chinese five spice

1 garlic clove, crushed

125 g (4½ oz) cooked peeled
  prawns, defrosted if frozen

125 g (4½ oz) beansprouts

4 spring onions, shredded

1 tablespoon light soy sauce

8 x 15 g (½ oz) filo pastry
  sheets, measuring
  30 x 40 cm (12 x 16 inches),
  defrosted if frozen

2 tablespoons sunflower oil

1 teaspoon sesame seeds

These are rather like spring rolls, but with a lot less calories. Serve with a drizzle of soy sauce.

1 Place the sesame oil, Chinese five spice and garlic in a bowl. Add the prawns and toss together well.

2 Place the beansprouts, spring onions and soy sauce in a small lidded saucepan, cover with a tight fitting lid and cook for 2–3 minutes until wilted. Drain and toss with the prawn mixture.

3 Preheat the oven to Gas Mark 5/190°C/fan oven 170°C. Line a baking tray with non stick baking parchment.

4 Brush each filo pastry sheet with sunflower oil. Place a spoonful of the prawn mixture on one side, fold the edges over and then roll up to enclose the filling. Transfer to the prepared baking tray, seam side down.

5 Sprinkle with the sesame seeds and bake for 10–12 minutes, until the pastry is crisp. Serve hot.

🍏 **Variation...** If you prefer, make a vegetarian version by using a mixture of thin strips of carrot, courgette and baby corn instead of the prawns.

Warm chicken salad with lemon dressing

Serves 4

276 calories per serving

Takes 10 minutes to prepare,
15 minutes to cook

4 x 165 g (5¾ oz) skinless
boneless chicken breasts

175 g (6 oz) green beans,
trimmed

1 bag rocket or watercress

a large handful of baby
spinach leaves, washed

½ Iceberg lettuce, shredded

1 teaspoon finely grated
lemon zest

1 tablespoon lemon juice

1 tablespoon white wine
vinegar or rice vinegar

2 tablespoons olive oil

1 teaspoon Dijon mustard

salt and freshly ground black
pepper

*You can buy so many delicious salad leaves these days,
which give such great flavour to your salads.*

1 Preheat the grill to medium-high and grill the chicken breasts,
turning once, until cooked; they will take about 15 minutes.

2 At the same time, bring a saucepan of water to the boil, add
the green beans and cook until just tender, about 4 minutes.
Drain, refresh in cold water and drain well again.

3 Meanwhile, rinse all the salad leaves and arrange in four
serving bowls. Mix together the lemon zest, lemon juice,
vinegar, olive oil and mustard and season.

4 Slice the hot chicken and divide between the salads with the
green beans. Spoon the dressing over each portion and serve
at once.

Variation... Use a couple of bags of mixed salad leaves
instead of the rocket or watercress, spinach and Iceberg
lettuce.

Spicy stuffed mushrooms

Serves 4

90 calories per serving

Takes 30 minutes to prepare,
25–30 minutes to cook

Ⓥ

60 g (2 oz) dried basmati rice

½ teaspoon turmeric

4 large Portobello or flat mushrooms, peeled

calorie controlled cooking spray

4 spring onions, chopped

1 garlic clove, crushed

2 large tomatoes, sliced thickly

70 g (2¾ oz) fresh or frozen peas

½ tablespoon chopped fresh flat leaf parsley, plus extra sprigs, to garnish

1 teaspoon medium curry powder

salt and freshly ground black pepper

This colourful dish will brighten up any dinner table. It's also a lovely accompaniment to grilled steak and salad.

1 Bring a saucepan of water to the boil and add the rice and turmeric. Cook for 20 minutes or according to the packet instructions. Preheat the oven to Gas Mark 6/200°C/fan oven 180°C.

2 Carefully remove the stalks from the mushrooms. Chop the stalks and reserve them. Place the mushrooms in a small roasting tin.

3 A few minutes before the rice is ready, spray a small non stick saucepan with the cooking spray and fry the spring onions, garlic and mushroom stalks for a couple of minutes. Select the best four slices of tomato and put them to one side. Dice the remaining tomato and add it to the frying pan with the peas, parsley and curry powder. Season.

4 Drain the rice thoroughly and add to the pan. Heat through for a minute or so, making sure everything is well mixed.

5 Spoon the rice mixture into the mushrooms, firmly pushing it down, and top each mushroom with a slice of tomato. Spray with the cooking spray and bake in the oven for 25–30 minutes or until the mushrooms are tender. Serve immediately, garnished with the remaining sprigs of parsley.

Tip... Wide, deep mushrooms are the easiest to stuff. To show off the colourful stuffing, choose tomatoes that are 2 cm (¾ inch) smaller in diameter than the mushrooms.

Spicy crab cakes

Serves 4

123 calories per serving

Takes 30 minutes to prepare
+ 20 minutes chilling,
12–16 minutes to cook

150 g (5½ oz) potatoes, peeled
250 g (9 oz) crab meat
3 spring onions, sliced
½ teaspoon cayenne pepper
1 teaspoon wholegrain mustard
½ red pepper, de-seeded and chopped finely
grated zest and juice of ½ a lime
1 tablespoon chopped fresh coriander
calorie controlled cooking spray
salt and freshly ground black pepper

These tasty crab cakes are perfect for a light lunch or served as a starter for a dinner party for friends. Serve with a green salad.

1 Bring a small saucepan of water to the boil, add the potatoes and cook for 8–10 minutes until tender. Drain and leave to cool.

2 Place the remaining ingredients, except the cooking spray, in a bowl.

3 When the potatoes are cool enough to handle, grate them into the bowl.

4 Mix well and shape into eight crab cakes. Place on a plate or tray and chill for 20 minutes.

5 Heat a large non stick frying pan, spray with the cooking spray and add the crab cakes. Cook for 3–4 minutes on each side and serve immediately.

Oven roasted tomato tartlets

Serves 8

191 calories per serving

Takes 15 minutes to prepare,
1¼ hours to cook

Ⓥ

❄ (roasted tomatoes only)

1 kg (2 lb 4 oz) plum tomatoes,
  halved horizontally
1 teaspoon salt
8 x 45 g (1½ oz) filo pastry
  sheets, measuring
  50 x 24 cm (20 x 9½ inches)
2 tablespoons olive oil
2 tablespoons torn fresh basil
  leaves (optional)
freshly ground black pepper

Simple but very effective tartlets that are perfect for a starter.

1 Preheat the oven to Gas Mark 2/150°C/fan oven 130°C.

2 Arrange the tomatoes cut side up on a cooling rack. Place the cooling rack over a baking tray and then sprinkle the salt over the tomatoes.

3 Roast the tomatoes in the oven for 1 hour, until they are beginning to dry out a little. Remove the tomatoes from the oven and increase the oven temperature to Gas Mark 5/190°C/fan oven 170°C.

4 Cut each sheet of filo pastry in half, brush with a little of the oil and place the two halves together with the corners at angles to each other – not neatly lined up in a square. Gently press into eight individual tartlet tins, scrunching up the edges with your fingers so the pastry fits into the tins. Brush the insides of the tartlet cases with any remaining oil. Bake for 10–15 minutes, until the pastry is crisp and golden.

5 Remove the pastry cases from the oven, lift carefully from the tins and place on serving plates. Fill with the roasted tomato halves. Scatter each tartlet with a little torn basil, if using, and a generous grinding of black pepper.

Gourmet beef burger

Serves 6

330 calories per serving

Takes 25 minutes to prepare
  + chilling

**600 g (1 lb 5 oz) lean steak
mince**

**1 tablespoon dried thyme or
mixed herbs**

**calorie controlled cooking
spray**

2 onions, sliced thinly

**salt and freshly ground black
pepper**

To serve

a handful of lettuce leaves

**3 x 60 g (2 oz) crusty rolls,
halved**

6 tablespoons tomato relish

*Sometimes you just fancy something yummy – well here it
is in lean form but with all the flavour and juiciness.*

1 Place the mince in a bowl with the thyme or mixed herbs and
season. Mix well and shape into six large burgers, squeezing
the mixture together with your hands. Transfer to a plate and
chill for 10 minutes.

2 Spray a non stick frying pan with the cooking spray and heat
until hot. Add the onions and cook over a medium-high heat
for 5–10 minutes until golden and crispy. You may need to add
a tablespoon or two of water to prevent them from sticking.
Remove from the pan and keep warm.

3 Respray the pan with the cooking spray and heat until hot.
Add the burgers and cook for 10 minutes, turning occasionally,
until browned and cooked through.

4 To serve, place a lettuce leaf on each half roll, add a burger,
top with a tablespoon of the relish and finally add the crispy
onions. Serve immediately.

Variation... You can also use the same amount of lamb
mince, instead of steak mince to make the burgers.

Toad in the hole

Serves 4

354 calories per serving

Takes 20 minutes to prepare,
45 minutes to cook

1 tablespoon sunflower oil
450 g (1 lb) low fat pork sausages
225 g (8 oz) carrots, peeled and cut into thick chunks
1 red onion, cut into wedges
4 celery sticks, cut into 5 cm (2 inch) pieces

For the batter

100 g (3½ oz) plain flour
a pinch of salt
1 egg
300 ml (10 fl oz) skimmed milk
1 teaspoon dried mixed herbs

The vegetables in this popular dish add a burst of colour. They also make it a more filling meal.

1 Preheat the oven to Gas Mark 6/200°C/fan oven 180°C. Place the oil in a 23 cm (9 inch) square non stick baking tin or ovenproof dish. Arrange the sausages, carrots, onion and celery in the base of the tin or dish and roast in the oven for 20 minutes.

2 Meanwhile, make the batter. Sift the flour and salt into a mixing bowl and make a well in the centre. Add the egg, milk and herbs and whisk to form a smooth batter.

3 Remove the sausages and vegetables from the oven and pour over the batter. Return the tin to the oven for 20–25 minutes until the batter is well risen and deep golden.

4 Cut the toad in the hole into quarters and serve hot.

Variation... Try using other vegetables for this dish, such as open cup mushrooms or chunks of leeks or courgettes.

Lemon and honey lamb steaks

Serves 4

332 calories per serving

Takes 35 minutes to prepare
  + 20 minutes marinating

**4 x 125 g (4½ oz) lean lamb
  leg steaks, visible fat
  removed**

**grated zest and juice of a
  small lemon**

1 tablespoon runny honey

450 g (1 lb) new potatoes

**leaves from 2 lemon thyme
  sprigs**

**salt and freshly ground black
  pepper**

*Marinating these steaks for as little as 20 minutes makes
them incredibly flavourful. Serve with steamed green beans.*

1 Place the lamb in a non metallic bowl. Mix together the
lemon zest and juice with the honey and pour over the lamb,
ensuring it is thoroughly coated. Set aside, uncovered, to
marinate for 20 minutes.

2 Bring a saucepan of water to the boil, add the potatoes and
simmer for 10–15 minutes until tender. Reserve 2 tablespoons
of the potato cooking liquid and then drain the potatoes and
lightly crush them using the back of a spoon. Add the reserved
cooking liquid, lemon thyme leaves and a little seasoning.
Keep warm.

3 Preheat the grill to medium. Remove the lamb from the
marinade and grill for 8–10 minutes, turning once, until cooked
through and beginning to char.

4 In a saucepan, boil the remaining marinade for 1–2 minutes,
until thickened.

5 Serve the lamb with the marinade drizzled over and
accompanied by the potatoes.

Tip... Lemon thyme looks similar to ordinary thyme but
has a fresh lemon flavour. If you can't find it, use ordinary
thyme instead.

Stuffed lamb with turnip bake

Serves 6
460 calories per serving
Takes 30 minutes to prepare, 1¼ hours to cook

calorie controlled cooking spray
750 g (1 lb 9 oz) boned shoulder of lamb
salt and freshly ground black pepper

For the stuffing
125 g (4½ oz) ready to eat apricots, chopped
75 g (2¾ oz) fresh breadcrumbs
a small bunch of fresh rosemary, chopped
grated zest and juice of a lemon

For the turnip bake
1 onion, sliced finely
a few fresh thyme sprigs, chopped, plus some
  to serve
1.5 kg (3 lb 5 oz) turnips, peeled and sliced
  thinly
100 ml (3½ fl oz) vegetable stock
50 g (1¾ oz) half fat Cheddar cheese, grated

For the gravy
1 tablespoon plain flour
450 ml (16 fl oz) lamb or vegetable stock

A delicious and impressive dish for a special meal.

1 Preheat the oven to Gas Mark 6/200°C/fan oven 180°C. Spray a roasting tin with the cooking spray and lay the lamb, boned side up, in the tin.

2 In a bowl, mix together all the stuffing ingredients and season. Spread the stuffing over the lamb, leaving a small border all around. Roll up the lamb and secure with string. Put in the oven and roast for 1¼ hours.

3 Meanwhile, make the turnip bake. Spray a non stick frying pan with the cooking spray and stir fry the onion and thyme until softened, adding a splash of water if they start to stick.

4 Arrange a layer of turnips over the bottom of an ovenproof pan, large cake tin or round baking tray. Scatter with the fried onions and add another layer of turnips, more onions and so on until both are used up.

5 Pour over the vegetable stock and then sprinkle over the Cheddar cheese. Cover the pan or tin with foil and place in the oven with the lamb for 1 hour. When it's ready, use the tip of a knife to loosen around the edges of the pan and then tip out the turnip bake like a cake, upside down, on to a serving plate. Scatter with the extra thyme and keep warm until ready to serve.

6 Remove the lamb from the roasting tin, place on a carving board, cover with foil and leave to rest while you make the gravy.

7 Pour away any fat in the roasting tin and heat the tin on the hob over a high heat. Add the flour and stir into the stuck on juices in the pan with a wooden spoon. Gradually add the stock, stirring vigorously and scraping any juices and flour off the bottom of the tin. Boil for 3–4 minutes until thickened. Season to taste and pour into a serving jug. Serve with the lamb and turnip bake.

Beef Wellington

Serves 4

436 calories per serving

Takes 40 minutes to prepare,
45 minutes to cook

25 g (1 oz) dried mixed
mushrooms

¼ kettleful of boiling water

calorie controlled cooking
spray

1 red onion, chopped finely

2 garlic cloves, crushed

75 g (2¾ oz) chestnut
mushrooms, chopped finely

1 tablespoon fresh thyme
leaves

2 tablespoons low fat soft
cheese

450 g (1 lb) lean beef fillet

200 g (7 oz) ready rolled puff
pastry, cut into a 20 x 23 cm
(8 x 9 inch) rectangle

1 egg, beaten

salt and freshly ground black
pepper

Served with steamed sugar snap peas and carrots.

1 Put the dried mushrooms in a small bowl and cover with boiling water. Set aside to soak.

2 Heat a non stick frying pan and spray with the cooking spray. Add the onion, garlic, chestnut mushrooms and 2 tablespoons of the mushroom soaking liquid and cook for 10 minutes. Remove from the heat.

3 Drain the dried mushrooms and chop finely. Stir into the cooked mushroom mixture with the thyme and soft cheese. Season and leave for about 10 minutes to go cold.

4 Meanwhile, heat a non stick frying pan until hot and spray with the cooking spray. Cook the beef for 1 minute on each side to brown. Remove and set aside for 10 minutes.

5 Preheat the oven to Gas Mark 6/200°C/fan oven 180°C. Roll out the pastry to measure 23 x 25 cm (9 x 10 inches). Lay the beef fillet along one side, leaving a 2.5 cm (1 inch) border, and top with the mushroom mixture.

6 Brush around the beef with the egg and fold over the pastry to enclose the beef. Seal the edges, trimming where necessary. Brush with the remaining egg. Bake in the oven for 40–45 minutes until cooked.

Ham and sweetcorn lasagne

Serves 6

291 calories per serving

Takes 20 minutes to prepare
  + 15 minutes resting,
  45 minutes to cook

**calorie controlled cooking
  spray**
3 garlic cloves, crushed
2 teaspoons dried mixed herbs
**2 x 400 g cans chopped
  tomatoes**
175 g (6 oz) frozen sweetcorn
50 g (1¾ oz) cornflour
600 ml (20 fl oz) skimmed milk
**300 ml (10 fl oz) hot chicken
  stock**
2 bay leaves
**200 g (7 oz) wafer thin
  smoked ham, shredded**
**160 g (5½ oz) dried egg
  lasagne sheets**
**40 g (1½ oz) Parmesan
  cheese, grated**
freshly ground black pepper

Everyone loves lasagne, but it can be rather time-consuming. This version is quicker to prepare.

1 Preheat the oven to Gas Mark 4/180°C/fan oven 160°C. Heat a saucepan over a medium heat and spray with the cooking spray. Add the garlic and herbs and cook for 30 seconds before adding the tomatoes and simmering for 5 minutes. Add the sweetcorn, cook for 2 minutes and season with black pepper.

2 Meanwhile, place the cornflour in a non stick saucepan and gradually blend in the milk and stock. Add the bay leaves and bring to the boil, stirring until thickened. Simmer for 2 minutes and season with black pepper.

3 To assemble the lasagne, spread half the tomato sauce in the base of a large ovenproof baking dish and scatter over half the ham. Top with half the lasagne sheets and half the white sauce and then repeat the layers. Scatter the Parmesan all over the lasagne and cover with foil.

4 Bake for 30 minutes, remove the foil and increase the oven temperature to Gas Mark 6/200°C/fan oven 180°C. Cook for a further 15 minutes until nicely browned on top.

5 Remove from the oven and leave to rest for 15 minutes before serving, to allow the lasagne to firm up slightly and make it easier to serve.

🌱 **Variation...** Try a vegetarian of this recipe by using 200 g (7 oz) of Quorn Deli Ham Style Slices instead of the wafer thin smoked ham and replacing the chicken stock with vegetable stock.

White pork bourguignon

Serves 4
354 calories per serving
Takes 25 minutes to prepare,
2 hours to cook

1 tablespoon plain flour

750 g (1 lb 10 oz) boneless
pork shoulder, visible fat
removed and cut into
5 cm (2 inch) pieces

calorie controlled cooking
spray

1 onion, chopped finely

1 garlic clove, crushed

200 g (7 oz) chestnut
mushrooms

½ celeriac (about 350 g/12 oz),
peeled and cut into bite size
cubes

300 ml (10 fl oz) white
burgundy wine

300 ml (10 fl oz) chicken stock

1 dried bouquet garni

4 fresh thyme sprigs

salt and freshly ground black
pepper

Serve with a 125 g (4½ oz) scoop of mashed potato made up with 1 tablespoon of skimmed milk and 35 g (1¼ oz) of cooked broad beans per person.

1 Put the flour on a plate and dust the pork in it, shaking off the excess. Heat a lidded flameproof casserole dish and spray with the cooking spray. Cook the pork for 5 minutes, turning until brown all over. You may need to do this in batches. Remove to a plate and set aside.

2 Add the onion, garlic, mushrooms and celeriac to the dish and cook gently for 5 minutes until starting to brown. Return the pork and add the wine, chicken stock, bouquet garni and thyme. Bring to the boil, cover and simmer for 2 hours until the pork is tender and the juices have thickened. Remove the bouquet garni, check the seasoning and serve.

Tip... Make sure you use a good white wine from Burgundy to really make this dish special.

Pot roast

Serves 6

257 calories per serving

Takes 25 minutes to prepare,
   2 hours to cook

250 g (9 oz) small shallots

a kettleful of boiling water

700 g (1 lb 9 oz) lean
   silverside of beef, visible fat
   removed

6 x 15 g (½ oz) Parma ham
   slices

calorie controlled cooking
   spray

2 large garlic cloves

6 small fresh rosemary sprigs

2 tablespoons tomato purée

450 ml (16 fl oz) beef stock

25 g (1 oz) dried porcini
   mushrooms

2 fresh thyme sprigs

420 g can butter beans,
   drained and rinsed

Soaking the shallots in boiling water makes them easier to peel.

1 Preheat the oven to Gas Mark 3/160°C/fan oven 140°C. Put the shallots in a bowl, cover with boiling water and set aside.

2 Wrap the beef in the ham and spray with the cooking spray. Heat a large, lidded, flameproof and ovenproof casserole dish and cook the beef for 5 minutes, turning until brown all over. Remove to a large plate and set aside to cool.

3 Cut each garlic clove into six slivers. Make about twelve deep cuts in the top of the beef and fill each with a sliver of garlic and half a sprig of rosemary.

4 Drain and peel the shallots. Halve any that are large.

5 Heat the casserole dish again and spray with the cooking spray. Cook the shallots for 5 minutes until starting to soften and brown. Stir in the tomato purée and cook for 30 seconds. Stir in the stock, mushrooms, thyme and butter beans.

6 Return the beef to the casserole dish, nestling it into the beans. Bring to the boil, cover and then cook in the oven for 2 hours. To serve, remove the beef and carve it into slices, dividing it equally between six warmed plates. Spoon over the vegetables and pan juices.

Roast lamb with mint sauce

Serves 8
266 calories per serving
Takes 30 minutes to prepare
+ 15 minutes resting,
1½–1¾ hours to cook

2 kg (4 lb 8 oz) leg of lamb

6 fresh rosemary sprigs, snipped into smaller sprigs

4 garlic cloves, cut in half lengthways

calorie controlled cooking spray

100 ml (3½ fl oz) white wine

300 ml (10 fl oz) vegetable stock

salt and freshly ground black pepper

For the mint sauce

a bunch of fresh mint, leaves chopped

2 teaspoons caster sugar

3 tablespoons cider vinegar

4 tablespoons boiling water

A classic dish for a Sunday lunch. Serve with a selection of steamed vegetables.

1 Preheat the oven to Gas Mark 4/180°C/fan oven 160°C. Put the lamb in a roasting tin and, with a sharp knife, make small slits all over the surface of the lamb joint. Push the little sprigs of rosemary and pieces of garlic into these slits.

2 Season the joint well, spray with the cooking spray and roast for 1½–1¾ hours. Baste the joint every 30 minutes by spooning over the juices.

3 Meanwhile, make the mint sauce by mixing together all the ingredients until the sugar has dissolved. Keep in the fridge until you are ready to serve.

4 When the roast is cooked, lift from the roasting tin on to a carving board. Cover with foil and leave for 15 minutes before carving.

5 Meanwhile, make the gravy in the roasting tin. Pour the oil out of the tin and discard and then place the tin on the hob and heat. When sizzling, pour in the wine, scrape up all the browned bits from the base of the tin with a wooden spoon and stir well. Add the stock and bring to the boil, still scraping. Allow to bubble for a few minutes. Check the seasoning and strain into a jug.

6 Serve three 100 g (3½ oz) slices per person with the gravy and mint sauce.

Spanish ham and bean hotpot

Serves 4
231 calories per serving
Takes 25 minutes
❄

calorie controlled cooking
  spray
2 onions, chopped
250 g (9 oz) thick gammon
  steak, visible fat removed
  and cut into bite size chunks
2 large garlic cloves, chopped
2 teaspoons dried mixed herbs
400 g can chopped tomatoes
400 g can low sugar and low
  salt baked beans
½ teaspoon smoked paprika
salt and freshly ground black
  pepper

Smoked paprika gives this hearty hotpot a traditional Spanish flavour. Serve with a 50 g (1¾ oz) slice of crusty bread per person and lots of green vegetables, such as green beans.

1 Heat a large, lidded, non stick saucepan and spray with the cooking spray. Add the onions and cook, stirring, for 4 minutes, adding a splash of water if they start to stick. Add the gammon and cook for another 3 minutes. Stir in the garlic and cook for a further 1 minute.

2 Add the herbs, tomatoes, beans, paprika and 100 ml (3½ fl oz) of water and bring to the boil, stirring occasionally. Reduce the heat, season and simmer, half-covered, for 10 minutes until the sauce has thickened slightly.

3 Serve in warmed bowls.

Roast turkey with orange and mushroom stuffing

Serves 6

542 calories per serving as suggested

Takes 40 minutes to prepare + 30 minutes resting, 1–1½ hours to cook (depending on the turkey size)

1.5–2.25 kg (3½–5 lb) turkey
12 x 25 g (1 oz) streaky bacon rashers
425 ml (15 fl oz) chicken or turkey stock
calorie controlled cooking spray
salt and freshly ground black pepper

For the stuffing
300 ml (10 fl oz) boiling water
170 g packet parsley and thyme or garlic and herb stuffing mix
100 g (3½ oz) mushrooms, chopped
grated zest and juice of an orange

For the bread sauce
3 cloves
1 small onion, peeled
425 ml (15 fl oz) skimmed milk
1 bay leaf
4 peppercorns
6 medium slices white bread, crusts removed and cubed
freshly grated nutmeg

For the gravy
1 tablespoon plain flour
300 ml (10 fl oz) chicken or turkey stock

These are simple recipes for a succulent roast turkey with stuffing, gravy and a bread sauce. Using a few shortcuts you can enjoy a stress-free dinner.

1 Preheat the oven to Gas Mark 5/190°C/fan oven 170°C. Rinse the turkey, pat dry with kitchen towel and then season inside and out.

2 Pour the boiling water over the stuffing mix, add the mushrooms and orange zest and juice and stir well. Stuff the neck cavity of the turkey, using as much stuffing as necessary to give a good shape, without pressing in too much. Pull the flap of skin over the stuffing and tuck under the bird.

3 Weigh the turkey and then place in a large roasting tin. Stretch the bacon rashers, using the back of a knife, and place in a criss-cross pattern over the top of the bird. Pour the stock into the roasting tin and cover the turkey with a piece of foil that has been sprayed with the cooking spray.

4 To calculate the cooking time, allow 20 minutes per 500 g (1 lb 2 oz) of the weight of the stuffed bird – for example a 2 kg (4 lb 8 oz) stuffed turkey will take 1 hour and 20 minutes. Place the turkey in the centre of the oven and roast for the appropriate time, removing the foil for the last 30 minutes of the cooking time so that the bacon and skin become crisp.

5 Meanwhile, to make the bread sauce, stick the cloves into the onion and put in a large saucepan with the milk, bay leaf and peppercorns. Heat gently until the mixture comes to the boil. Remove from the heat and leave to infuse for at least an hour. Strain the milk and return to the pan. Put on a very low heat and add the bread and a couple of gratings of nutmeg. Season and cook for 10 minutes. Set aside. Reheat gently before use.

6 Check that the turkey is cooked by sticking a skewer or thin-bladed knife into the thickest part of the thigh; if the juices run clear then the bird is cooked, but if they look bloody then return to the oven for longer. Keep re-testing until they do run clear.

7 Transfer the turkey to a carving board, cover with foil and allow to rest for 30 minutes before carving. Meanwhile, place any leftover stuffing on a baking tray sprayed with the cooking spray and bake in the hot oven for 20 minutes.

8 To make the gravy, pour or skim any fat off the top of the juices left in the roasting tray, place the tray on the hob and heat. Stir in the flour, add the stock and bring to the boil, stirring with a wooden spoon and scraping up the juices stuck to the bottom of the pan. If the gravy looks lumpy then whisk and strain into a serving jug. Serve five 25 g (1 oz) slices of turkey per person with the stuffing, bread sauce and gravy.

Tip... When you eventually finish all the meat from your turkey, boil up the carcass with a little pepper, a bay leaf, a piece of carrot, onion and celery and enough water to cover. This makes a lovely stock to use in soups and risottos.

Stuffed chicken breasts with bacon

Serves 4

292 calories per serving

Takes 20 minutes to prepare,
30 minutes to cook

**calorie controlled cooking
spray**
4 garlic cloves, chopped finely
200 g (7 oz) frozen spinach
**4 x 150 g (5½ oz) skinless
boneless chicken breasts**
**8 x 25 g (1 oz) lean back
bacon rashers**
300 ml (10 fl oz) chicken stock
**salt and freshly ground black
pepper**

*A delicious chicken dish stuffed with spinach and garlic.
Serve with 60 g (2 oz) of dried tagliatelle per person,
cooked according to the packet instructions.*

1 Heat a lidded non stick frying pan, spray with the cooking
spray and fry the garlic for 2 minutes, until golden.

2 Turn the heat down, add the frozen spinach and cover the
pan. After 5 minutes, remove the lid and stir to break up any
lumps of spinach. Season. Continue to cook gently until the
spinach is completely heated through. Preheat the oven to Gas
Mark 4/180°C/fan oven 160°C.

3 Season the chicken breasts and then slice into the thickest
side to make a pocket. Stuff with the spinach and wrap each
breast in two slices of bacon to cover the flesh completely.

4 Lay the chicken breasts in a non stick roasting tin and spray
with the cooking spray. Pour the stock into the tin and cook
for 30 minutes until golden and crisp on the top and cooked
through.

5 Serve the chicken breasts with the juices from the pan.

Mexican chicken tortillas

Serves 4
597 calories per serving
Takes 40 minutes

8 x 40 g (1½ oz) soft flour tortillas

660 g (1 lb 8 oz) skinless boneless chicken breasts, cut into thin strips

150 ml (5 fl oz) low fat natural yogurt

4 medium slices bread, processed to fine breadcrumbs

calorie controlled cooking spray

salt and freshly ground black pepper

For the salsa

500 g (1lb 2 oz) frozen petit pois

100 g (3½ oz) cherry tomatoes, quartered

1 small red onion, chopped finely

juice of a lime

1 small red chilli, de-seeded and chopped

A fun and satisfying dinner.

1 Preheat the oven to Gas Mark 4/180°C/fan oven 160°C. Wrap the tortillas in foil and place in the oven to heat through.

2 Meanwhile, place the chicken strips in a bowl, season and then toss in the yogurt until well covered. Place the breadcrumbs on a plate and roll the chicken strips in them until coated.

3 Heat a large non stick frying pan and spray with the cooking spray. Add the chicken strips and fry the chicken for 4–5 minutes, turning gently until golden brown all over and cooked through.

4 Meanwhile, bring a small saucepan of water to the boil, add the petit pois and cook for 5 minutes. Drain thoroughly and set aside.

5 Arrange large spoonfuls of the chicken on the centre of the warmed tortillas and roll up.

6 Place all the ingredients for the salsa, including the peas, in a food processor, season and blend very briefly to a rough textured paste. Alternatively, mash the ingredients together with a fork. Transfer to a bowl and serve with the tortillas.

Turkey terrine

Serves 6

242 calories per serving

Takes 20 minutes to prepare,
1 hour to cook

**10 x 15 g (½ oz) Parma ham
slices**
450 g (1 lb) lean turkey mince
4 egg yolks
250 g (9 oz) Quark
**1 tablespoon mixed
peppercorns in brine,
drained**
1 tablespoon dried tarragon
a kettleful of boiling water

*Serve with 150 g (5½ oz) of cooked new potatoes, tossed
with 2 teaspoons of olive oil and 1 tablespoon of chopped
parsley, and pickled gherkins and pickled onions.*

1 Preheat the oven to Gas Mark 3/160°C/fan oven 140°C. Line
a 900 g (2 lb) loaf tin with the slices of Parma ham, ensuring
that the joins overlap, that there are no gaps and leaving the
ends overhanging the edge of the tin.

2 In a large bowl, mix together the turkey mince, egg yolks,
Quark, peppercorns and tarragon until combined. Spoon into
the loaf tin, pressing down with the back of a spoon. Fold the
overhanging lengths of Parma ham back over the meat to
wrap up.

3 Put the loaf tin in a roasting tray and fill the tray two thirds
of the way up the sides of the loaf tin with boiling water. Bake
in the oven for 1 hour or until the juices run clear.

4 Drain the water away from the tin and turn the loaf out on
to a plate. Wipe away the milky residue with damp kitchen
towel. Carve into slices and serve warm or leave to go cold
and then slice.

Chicken tagine

Serves 4

284 calories per serving

Takes 5 minutes to prepare,
1½ hours to cook

**4 x 175 g (6 oz) skinless
chicken breasts**

2 onions, chopped

2 cinnamon sticks

½ teaspoon ground ginger

½ teaspoon ground coriander

**250 g (9 oz) canned prunes in
natural juice, drained**

1 tablespoon honey

**salt and freshly ground black
pepper**

*This North African dish is named after the pot with a tall,
conical lid in which it is traditionally cooked. Serve with
60 g (2 oz) of dried rice or 60 g (2 oz) of dried couscous
per person, cooked according to the packet instructions.*

1 Put the chicken in a large lidded saucepan with the onions
and cinnamon sticks. Sprinkle with the ginger and coriander,
season and then cover with water. Simmer gently, covered, for
1 hour.

2 Add the prunes and honey and cook for a further 30 minutes,
uncovered, until the prunes are soft and the sauce has reduced
considerably.

Variation... Instead of prunes, use apricots or peeled,
cored and chopped cooking apples. If using apples, add
15 minutes before the end of the cooking time. It's best
to use cooking apples because they will not disintegrate
as easily when they are cooked.

Duck breasts with pepper sauce

Serves 4

210 calories per serving

Takes 25 minutes

calorie controlled cooking
   spray

4 x 125 g (4 oz) skinless
   boneless duck breasts,
   visible fat removed

1 red onion, diced

2 tablespoons green
   peppercorns

100 ml (3½ fl oz) chicken
   stock

4 tablespoons low fat fromage
   frais

*This wonderfully rich creamy sauce goes well with
succulent duck breasts for a special occasion. Serve
accompanied by vegetables of your choice.*

1 Heat a non stick frying pan and spray with the cooking
spray. Cook the duck breasts for 5–6 minutes on each side,
depending on how rare you like your meat. Remove from the
pan and keep warm.

2 Add the onion to the pan and cook for 2–3 minutes before
adding the remaining ingredients. Simmer for 3–4 minutes.

3 Slice the duck breasts and serve with the sauce poured over.

Sunday chicken

Serves 8

356 calories per serving

Takes 10 minutes to prepare,
50 minutes to cook

calorie controlled cooking
spray

8 x 75 g (2¾ oz) skinless
boneless chicken thighs

8 x 75 g (2¾ oz) skinless
chicken drumsticks

4 leeks, sliced thinly

2 lemons, cut into quarters

4 fresh rosemary sprigs

850 ml (1½ pints) hot chicken
stock

600 g (1 lb 5 oz) potatoes,
peeled and diced

450 g (1 lb) parsnips, peeled
and diced

salt and freshly ground black
pepper

*This is a great one pot Sunday roast. Serve with steamed
broccoli and carrots.*

1 Preheat the oven to Gas Mark 6/200°C/fan oven 180°C.
Spray a large non stick frying pan with the cooking spray and
heat until hot. Add all the chicken and cook for 2–3 minutes,
turning until each piece is brown all over. You may have to do
this in batches. Remove from the heat.

2 Place the leeks in the bottom of a large roasting tin or divide
between two smaller tins. Top with the chicken and any pan
juices and the lemon quarters and rosemary. Pour over the stock.
Scatter over the potatoes and parsnips and spray liberally with
the cooking spray. Season.

3 Roast for 40–50 minutes until the chicken and vegetables
are tender. When a skewer is inserted into a drumstick the
juices should run clear. Serve immediately.

Variation... Swap the parsnips for the same quantity of
peeled and diced sweet potato for a change.

Balsamic roasted chicken

Serves 4

207 calories per serving

Takes 10 minutes to prepare,
25 minutes to cook

**calorie controlled cooking
spray**

**4 x 150 g (5½ oz) skinless
boneless chicken breasts**

1 large onion, quartered

**2 red peppers, de-seeded and
sliced into thin strips**

**1 green pepper, de-seeded
and sliced into thin strips**

2 garlic cloves, crushed

**4 tablespoons balsamic
vinegar**

**100 ml (3½ fl oz) chicken or
vegetable stock**

**a small bunch of fresh
oregano or 1 teaspoon dried
oregano**

**salt and freshly ground black
pepper**

*Serve with 60 g (2 oz) of dried pasta such as tagliatelle
or linguine per person, cooked according to the packet
instructions.*

1 Preheat the oven to Gas Mark 4/180°C/fan oven 160°C.
Spray a roasting tin with the cooking spray, place the chicken
breasts in the tin and season.

2 Spray a large non stick frying pan with the cooking spray
and stir fry the onion for a few minutes until it is softened,
adding a splash of water if it starts to stick. Add the peppers
and garlic, stir fry for a further minute and then tip the mixture
over the chicken breasts in the roasting tin.

3 Drizzle over the balsamic vinegar and stock, sprinkle with
the herbs and then roast in the oven for 20 minutes or until
cooked through. Halfway through, spoon some of the sauce
over the chicken breasts.

4 Check that the chicken is cooked and serve.

Fragrant chicken curry

Serves 4

216 calories per serving

Takes 20 minutes to prepare,
 10 minutes to cook

❄

calorie controlled cooking
 spray

**600 g (1 lb 5 oz) skinless
 boneless chicken breasts,
 cut into bite size pieces**

**1 red pepper, de-seeded and
 sliced finely**

**30 g (1¼ oz) fresh root ginger,
 grated**

2 garlic cloves, crushed

2 freeze dried lime leaves

**1 teaspoon mild or hot chilli
 powder**

**1 tablespoon mild curry
 powder**

**50 g (1¾ oz) low fat soft
 cheese**

**400 g can chopped tomatoes
 with herbs**

150 ml (5 fl oz) chicken stock

**75 g (2¾ oz) mange tout,
 shredded finely lengthways,
 to serve**

*A fast but effective recipe that is perfect for a spontaneous
supper with friends.*

1 Heat a deep non stick saucepan and spray with the cooking
spray. Add the chicken pieces and cook for 5 minutes until
brown all over. You may need to do this in batches. Remove
and set aside.

2 Spray the pan with the cooking spray again and add the
pepper, ginger, garlic and lime leaves. Cook for 1 minute. Stir
in the chilli powder and curry powder and return the chicken
to the pan, stirring constantly for 1 minute.

3 Add the soft cheese, tomatoes and stock. Bring to the
boil and simmer gently for 10 minutes until thickened and
the chicken is cooked. Serve immediately, topped with the
shredded mange tout.

❤ **Variation...** For a vegetarian option, use a 250 g packet
of tofu, diced, instead of the chicken, and vegetable stock
instead of chicken stock.

Chicken b'stilla roll

Serves 4

251 calories per serving

Takes 20 minutes to prepare
+ 10 minutes cooling,
45 minutes to cook

4 eggs

½ x 25 g packet fresh flat leaf parsley, chopped roughly

½ x 25 g packet fresh coriander, chopped roughly

1 preserved lemon from a jar, drained, pips removed and diced finely

350 g (12 oz) cooked skinless chicken breast, shredded

a generous pinch of saffron

1 tablespoon cornflour

8 x 15 g (½ oz) filo pastry sheets, measuring 30 x 40 cm (12 x 16 inches)

calorie controlled cooking spray

15 g (½ oz) flaked almonds

freshly ground black pepper

This is a fabulous chicken version of the B'stilla roll on page 130.

1 Preheat the oven to Gas Mark 4/180°C/fan oven 160°C. Put 3 eggs into a small saucepan, cover with water and bring to the boil. Simmer for 8 minutes and then drain and plunge into cold water.

2 Meanwhile, in a large bowl, mix together the parsley, coriander, diced lemon, chicken, saffron and freshly ground black pepper.

3 Dissolve the cornflour in 2 tablespoons of cold water to make a paste. Peel the eggs and chop roughly. Stir into the chicken mixture with the cornflour paste.

4 Lay a sheet of filo pastry on a non stick baking tray and spray with the cooking spray. Take a second filo sheet and lay it next to the first, overlapping one long edge slightly to make a rectangle measuring 30 x 25 cm (12 x 10 inches). Spray again with the cooking spray and repeat the layering until all the sheets are used.

5 Spread the chicken mixture over the rectangle leaving a 2.5 cm (1 inch) border all the way around. Spray the exposed filo pastry with the cooking spray and fold over the pastry of the two short sides. Roll up the pastry starting from one long side like a big Swiss roll.

6 Beat the remaining egg and brush over the pastry. Sprinkle with the almonds and bake in the oven for 40–45 minutes until golden. Leave to cool for 10 minutes and then cut into four and serve immediately.

Fish and seafood

Seafood and parsley tart

Serves 4

244 calories per serving

Takes 40 minutes to prepare
+ 30 minutes chilling,
30 minutes to cook

For the pastry

50 g (1¾ oz) low fat spread
100 g (3½ oz) plain flour
a pinch of salt
1 egg white, beaten

For the filling

**calorie controlled cooking
spray**
**4 shallots or 1 large onion,
chopped**
4 garlic cloves, chopped
**200 g (7 oz) mixed cooked
seafood, defrosted if frozen**
50 ml (2 fl oz) dry white wine
**a small bunch of fresh parsley,
chopped**
2 eggs, beaten
150 ml (5 fl oz) skimmed milk
**salt and freshly ground black
pepper**

A healthier version of a classic French tart.

1 Make the pastry by rubbing the low fat spread into the flour and salt until the mixture resembles fresh breadcrumbs. Add 1 tablespoon of water and quickly bring together into a ball with your hand. Wrap in cling film and chill for 30 minutes.

2 Preheat the oven to Gas Mark 6/200°C/fan oven 180°C. Roll out the pastry to a circle about 5 mm (¼ inch) thick and use to line a 19 cm (7½ inch) loose bottomed flan tin. Line with foil or non stick baking parchment and fill with baking beans.

3 Bake blind for 15 minutes and then remove the beans and lining, brush the case with the beaten egg white and bake for a further 10 minutes or until evenly golden brown. Remove from the oven and reduce the oven temperature to Gas Mark 5/190°C/fan oven 170°C.

4 Heat a large non stick saucepan, spray with the cooking spray and fry the shallots or onion and garlic for about 4 minutes until softened. Add the seafood with the white wine and parsley and stir.

5 Remove from the heat and stir in the eggs and milk and season. Pour into the pastry case and bake for 25–30 minutes, until just set and lightly browned.

Tips... To save time, you could use ready made shortcrust pastry.

Baking beans are ceramic beans that are readily available in cook shops and large supermarkets. If you don't have any, use dried beans or rice instead.

Lemon salmon en croûte

Serves 4

500 calories per serving

Takes 20 minutes to prepare,
25–30 minutes to cook

**250 g (9 oz) low fat soft
cheese**

**1 tablespoon chopped fresh
dill**

**1 tablespoon chopped fresh
parsley**

**grated zest and juice of a
lemon**

**8 x 15 g (½ oz) filo pastry
sheets, measuring
30 x 40 cm (12 x 16 inches)**

**calorie controlled cooking
spray**

**4 x 110 g (4 oz) salmon fillets,
skinned**

**salt and freshly ground black
pepper**

*Individual parcels are always impressive to serve up and
these are quick to make.*

1 Preheat the oven to Gas Mark 5/190°C/fan oven 170°C. Line
a baking tray with non stick baking parchment.

2 Mix the soft cheese with the herbs and lemon zest and juice
and season.

3 Spray a sheet of filo pastry with the cooking spray and top
with another sheet. Place a piece of salmon in the middle and
top with a quarter of the cheese mixture. Fold over the edges
like a parcel and spray with the cooking spray. Transfer to the
baking tray and repeat to make four parcels.

4 Bake for 25–30 minutes until the salmon is cooked through
and the pastry is golden.

Tips... Make these parcels up to 2 hours in advance and
refrigerate.

If you have time, marinate the salmon in the lemon juice
and herbs for 30 minutes beforehand, mixing any remaining
marinade with the soft cheese.

Luxurious smoked salmon pasta

Serves 4

362 calories per serving

Takes 5 minutes to prepare,
  15 minutes to cook

**240 g (8½ oz) dried pasta
  shapes or ribbons**

**300 g (10½ oz) smoked
  salmon, cut into bite size
  pieces**

½ cucumber, diced finely

**grated zest and juice of a
  lemon**

**150 g (5½ oz) very low fat
  natural yogurt**

**50 g (1¾ oz) low fat soft
  cheese**

25 g packet fresh dill, chopped

**salt and freshly ground black
  pepper**

A fast but rather special pasta dish.

1 Bring a saucepan of water to the boil, add the pasta and
cook for 10–15 minutes or according to the packet instructions.
Drain.

2 Add all the other ingredients to the drained pasta, toss
together and serve.

Marinated sardines with tomato relish

Serves 6

323 calories per serving

Takes 20 minutes to prepare
+ marinating, 5 minutes
to cook

**12 x 90 g (3¼ oz) sardines,
gutted**

For the marinade

**1½ tablespoons chopped fresh
coriander**

**1½ tablespoons chopped fresh
parsley**

3 garlic cloves, crushed

1 teaspoon ground cumin

1 teaspoon ground coriander

2 teaspoons paprika

a pinch of saffron threads

a pinch of dried chilli flakes

grated zest and juice of a lemon

For the relish

4 spring onions

juice of a lime

**250 g (9 oz) tomatoes, skinned,
de-seeded and chopped**

**½ dried red chilli, de-seeded
and chopped**

**3 tablespoons chopped fresh
coriander**

*A fantastic way to serve fish all through the year, but
especially in the summer when they can be popped on the
barbecue.*

1 To make the marinade, mix all the ingredients together in a
bowl.

2 Put the sardines in a non metallic dish and pour over the
marinade. Turn the fish so that they are completely coated in
the marinade and set aside in the fridge for at least 1 hour.

3 To make the relish, place all the ingredients in a blender, or
use a hand held blender, and whizz briefly to give a chunky
relish.

4 Heat the grill or barbecue to hot and cook the sardines for
3–4 minutes on each side. Serve immediately with the tomato
relish.

Tips... Sardines smaller than about 13 cm (5 inches) long
do not need to be gutted.

You can make the relish earlier and store it in the fridge,
but leave it to come to room temperature out of the fridge
while you cook the sardines.

Fish stew

Serves 6

287 calories per serving

Takes 20 minutes to prepare,
35 minutes to cook

2 teaspoons olive oil

2 onions, sliced

450 g (1 lb) pumpkin or
butternut squash, peeled,
de-seeded and cut into small
cubes

1 litre (1¾ pints) chicken or
vegetable stock

450 g (1 lb) floury potatoes,
peeled

200 ml (7 fl oz) dry white wine

250 g (9 oz) frozen sweetcorn

300 g (10½ oz) smoked
haddock fillets, skinned and
cut into chunks

300 g (10½ oz) haddock fillets,
skinned and cut into chunks

a bunch of watercress,
shredded, with a few sprigs
reserved to garnish

salt and freshly ground black
pepper

Tabasco sauce, to serve

*A soupy stew, thickened with floury potatoes. Serve in big
bowls, with a 50 g (1¾ oz) crusty roll per person.*

1 Heat the oil in a large non stick saucepan and gently fry the
onions for 5 minutes or until soft, adding a splash of water if
they start to stick.

2 Add the pumpkin or butternut squash, stock, potatoes and
wine and bring to the boil. Simmer for 30 minutes, or until the
potatoes have broken up and thickened the stew.

3 Add the sweetcorn together with both kinds of fish and the
watercress. Bring back to just below boiling and simmer very
gently for 5 minutes. Season and serve in warmed soup plates
or bowls with a dash of Tabasco sauce.

Quick Chinese cod

Serves 4
294 calories per serving
Takes 20 minutes

200 g (7 oz) dried fine egg noodles

calorie controlled cooking spray

1 courgette, cut into matchstick shapes

1 red pepper, de-seeded and cut into matchstick shapes

400 g can chopped tomatoes

½ teaspoon Chinese five spice

1 tablespoon soy sauce

450 g (1 lb) cod fillets, skinned and cut into bite size chunks

salt and freshly ground black pepper

This is a tasty but fast dish, with all the flavours of the Orient.

1 Bring a saucepan of water to the boil, add the noodles and cook according to the packet instructions. Drain and set aside.

2 Heat a large, lidded, non stick frying pan, spray with the cooking spray and fry the courgette and pepper for 3–4 minutes, until they start to soften.

3 Stir in the tomatoes, Chinese five spice, soy sauce and cod. Cover and cook for 5 minutes, until the fish starts to flake.

4 Stir in the drained noodles and season before serving.

Variations... You can omit the noodles from this recipe and serve with 200 g (7 oz) of dried basmati rice, cooked according to the packet instructions.

You can use any firm fish for this recipe. Hake, salmon, tuna and even swordfish are delicious alternatives.

Chilli seafood spaghetti

Serves 4

301 calories per serving

Takes 6 minutes to prepare,
  10 minutes to cook

200 g (7 oz) dried spaghetti
**calorie controlled cooking
  spray**
1 onion, chopped
¼ teaspoon chilli flakes
400 g can chopped tomatoes
**300 g (10½ oz) mixed cooked
  seafood, defrosted if frozen**
**2 tablespoons chopped fresh
  parsley**
**salt and freshly ground black
  pepper**
**50 g (1¾ oz) half fat Cheddar
  cheese, grated, to serve**

*A great pasta dish with a lovely spicy tomato and seafood
sauce.*

1 Bring a saucepan of water to the boil, add the pasta and
cook for 6–8 minutes, or according to the packet instructions,
until al dente.

2 Meanwhile, heat a large non stick pan, spray with the cooking
spray and sauté the onion for 3–4 minutes.

3 Add the chilli flakes, pour in the tomatoes and cook for
1–2 minutes. Add the mixed seafood, stir in the parsley and
heat through.

4 When the pasta is cooked, drain and add to the seafood
mixture. Toss gently to coat the pasta with the sauce, check
the seasoning and divide between four pasta bowls. Sprinkle
with the grated cheese and serve immediately.

Tip... If you like your food slightly hotter, just add more
chilli flakes.

Variation... This can be made into a more substantial meal
by adding 50 g (1¾ oz) of prawns or chopped salami.

Baked cod in a parcel

Serves 4

221 calories per serving

Takes 10 minutes to prepare,
20 minutes to cook

4 x 175 g (6 oz) cod fillets,
skinned

1 red pepper, de-seeded and
diced finely

1 red onion, diced finely

a small bunch of fresh
oregano, chopped

2 garlic cloves, chopped finely

2 tomatoes, chopped

juice of a lemon

1 tablespoon olive oil

4 tablespoons dry white wine
or balsamic vinegar

salt and freshly ground black
pepper

*The advantage of cooking fish in baking parchment is that
the fish cooks quickly and seals in all the flavours. Also,
opening the parcels up, as you do in this Portuguese recipe,
is an exciting way to start a meal.*

1 Preheat the oven to Gas Mark 6/200°C/fan oven 180°C.
Cut four pieces of non stick baking parchment, each measuring
30 cm (12 inches) square. Place a piece of fish in the middle of
each piece of paper, laying it diagonally from corner to corner.

2 In a bowl, mix together the pepper, onion, oregano, garlic,
tomatoes, lemon juice, olive oil and wine or vinegar. Season
well.

3 Spoon the mixture on top of the fish. Fold the parchment
over the fish to form a triangle. Fold the edges together tightly
to form a sealed parcel.

4 Lift the parcels on to a baking tray and bake for 15–20 minutes.
Place each parcel on a plate and serve at once, allowing each
guest to experience the cloud of fragrant steam that emerges
from the parcels.

Variation... This dish is equally delicious with trout, salmon,
seabass, haddock, coley or monkfish. Just use what is
freshest at the supermarket.

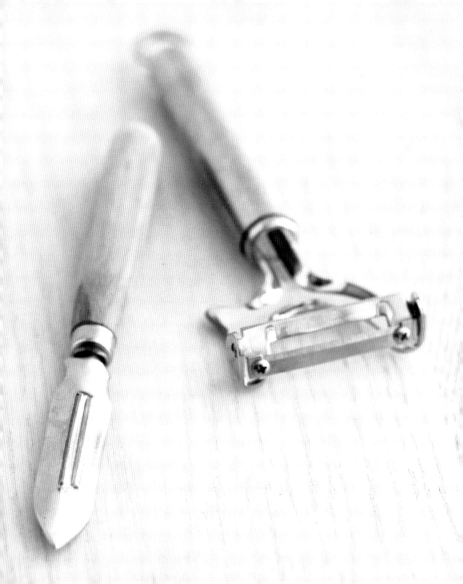

Simply vegetarian

Spring vegetable lasagne

Serves 4

322 calories per serving

Takes 35 minutes to prepare,
40 minutes to cook

Ⓥ

❄

calorie controlled cooking spray
6 spring onions, sliced
175 g (6 oz) carrots, peeled and diced
1 fennel bulb, sliced
110 g (4 oz) baby corn, halved
500 g (1 lb 2 oz) passata
2 garlic cloves, crushed
½ vegetable stock cube, crumbled
6–9 lasagne sheets (total weight 140 g/5 oz), fresh or no precook variety
8 cherry tomatoes, halved
40 g (1½ oz) mature Cheddar cheese, grated
salt and freshly ground black pepper

For the sauce
25 g (1 oz) low fat spread
25 g (1 oz) plain flour
450 ml (16 fl oz) skimmed milk

Lasagne is always a family favourite. Serve with a green salad.

1 Lightly spray a large non stick saucepan with the cooking spray and heat until hot. Add the spring onions, carrots, fennel and baby corn. Stir fry for 3 minutes. Add the passata, garlic and stock cube. Reduce the heat and simmer for 10 minutes until the vegetables are tender. Season.

2 Preheat the oven to Gas Mark 5/190°C/fan oven 170°C.

3 To make the sauce, melt the low fat spread in a small saucepan, add the flour and mix well. Cook for 1 minute and remove from the heat. Gradually add the milk, beating to a smooth paste after each addition before adding more. Return to the heat and cook gently, stirring continuously, until the sauce thickens, just coating the back of a spoon. Season.

4 Place a third of the vegetable mixture in the base of an ovenproof lasagne dish. Spoon over 2 tablespoons of the sauce and top with 2 or 3 (depending on their size) pasta sheets. Spoon half the remaining vegetable mixture on top of the pasta and top with half the remaining sauce and another 2 or 3 pasta sheets. Repeat with the remaining vegetable mixture and pasta. Spoon over the remaining sauce.

5 Scatter over the tomatoes, sprinkle with the cheese and bake for 40 minutes until golden and bubbling.

Tip... You can try other vegetables in the lasagne – broccoli or courgettes work well.

Spicy veggie balls in kefta sauce

Serves 4
198 calories per serving
Takes 1¼ hours

1 large red onion, chopped finely

150 ml (5 fl oz) hot vegetable stock

225 g (8 oz) Quorn mince

1 tablespoon chopped fresh mint

1 tablespoon chopped fresh parsley

½ teaspoon dried marjoram

75 g (2¾ oz) fresh breadcrumbs

1 egg, beaten

¼ teaspoon ground cumin

¼ teaspoon cayenne pepper

¼ teaspoon paprika

¼ teaspoon ground mixed spice

salt and freshly ground black pepper

For the sauce

3 x 400 g cans chopped tomatoes

1 red onion, chopped finely

1 tablespoon chopped fresh parsley

1 garlic clove, crushed

a pinch of salt, paprika and cayenne pepper

Serve these tasty veggie balls with 60 g (2 oz) of dried basmati rice per person, cooked according to the packet instructions.

1 First of all, make the kefta sauce. Put all the sauce ingredients into a large saucepan with 300 ml (10 fl oz) of water and simmer gently for 60–70 minutes.

2 Meanwhile, make the veggie balls. Put the onion and stock into a saucepan and simmer for 10 minutes, or until the liquid has just evaporated. Tip into a mixing bowl and allow to cool. Preheat the oven to Gas Mark 4/180°C/fan oven 160°C.

3 Add the Quorn to the onion with all the remaining ingredients. Stir well to combine and then shape into 12 balls.

4 Arrange in a roasting tin or baking dish in a single layer. Roast in the oven for 25–30 minutes, or until browned and crispy on the outside.

5 Put the cooked veggie balls into the sauce and simmer for 5 minutes before serving.

Spinach and four cheese cannelloni

Serves 6
278 calories per serving
Takes 25 minutes to prepare,
  25 minutes to cook
Ⓥ
❄

It's hard to believe it, but these baked cannelloni really do contain four cheeses: ricotta, Quark, Parmesan and mozzarella. Serve with a tomato and basil salad, drizzled with a little balsamic vinegar.

calorie controlled cooking spray
1 onion, chopped finely
2 garlic cloves, crushed
225 g (8 oz) frozen spinach
150 g (5½ oz) ricotta cheese
250 g (9 oz) Quark
25 g (1 oz) Parmesan cheese, grated
freshly grated nutmeg
18 dried cannelloni tubes
700 g (1 lb 9 oz) passata
125 g (4½ oz) light mozzarella cheese, drained and diced
1 tablespoon shredded fresh basil, plus whole fresh basil leaves, to serve
salt and freshly ground black pepper

1 Preheat the oven to Gas Mark 5/190°C/fan oven 170°C.

2 Heat a lidded non stick saucepan, spray with the cooking spray, add the onion and cook for 5 minutes until softened. Add the garlic and spinach, cover the pan and cook for 5 minutes, stirring occasionally, until the spinach is defrosted. Tip into a bowl and leave to cool slightly.

3 Stir the ricotta, Quark and half the Parmesan into the spinach mixture, add the nutmeg and seasoning to taste and then use this mixture to stuff the cannelloni tubes.

4 Pour a quarter of the passata over the base of a large ovenproof dish. Tuck the filled cannelloni into the dish and scatter the mozzarella over the top. Pour the remaining passata over the cannelloni and then add the shredded basil and remaining Parmesan. Bake for 25 minutes until bubbling hot. Serve three cannelloni per person, garnished with the fresh basil leaves.

Tip... The easiest way to fill the cannelloni is to use a piping bag, minus the nozzle. If you don't have one, improvise with a large plastic food bag – place the filling inside and fold over the top several times to close, then snip off a sealed corner and squeeze the filling into the cannelloni tubes.

Sweet potato roulade

Serves 6

196 calories per serving

Takes 30 minutes to prepare,
15 minutes to cook

Ⓥ

**600 g (1 lb 5 oz) sweet
potatoes, peeled and
chopped roughly**

**calorie controlled cooking
spray**

**225 g (8 oz) low fat soft
cheese with garlic and herbs**

**5 tablespoons low fat natural
yogurt**

**a bunch of spring onions,
chopped finely**

1 teaspoon ground coriander

4 eggs, separated

**1 tablespoon kalonji seeds
(optional)**

**salt and freshly ground black
pepper**

Sweet potato gives this roulade a glorious colour.

1 Bring a saucepan of water to the boil, add the sweet
potatoes, cook until tender and then drain.

2 Preheat the oven to Gas Mark 6/200°C/fan oven 180°C. Line
a 33 x 25 cm (13 x 10 inch) Swiss roll tin with non stick baking
parchment and spray with the cooking spray.

3 In a small bowl, mix together the soft cheese, yogurt and
spring onions. Set aside.

4 Place the cooked sweet potatoes in a food processor with
the coriander and blend until smooth. Add the egg yolks, season
and pulse to mix in. Remove to a bowl.

5 In a clean, grease-free bowl, whisk the egg whites until stiff
peaks form. Stir a large spoonful into the sweet potato mixture
before folding in the rest with a large metal spoon. Pour the
mixture into the tin, tipping it to get it into the corners and
smoothing with a palette knife. Bake for 10–15 minutes.

6 Meanwhile, lay a large sheet of non stick baking parchment
on the work surface over a clean tea towel. Sprinkle over the
kalonji seeds, if using.

7 When the roulade is cooked, tip it on to the baking parchment
and then roll it up, using the tea towel to help, and leave to cool.
When cool, gently unroll, spread with the cheese filling and roll
up again. Cut into slices to serve.

Tip... Kalonji or nigella seeds have a slightly peppery
flavour. You can find them in Asian stores.

Filo vegetable pie

Serves 6

287 calories per serving

Takes 30 minutes to prepare,
40 minutes to cook

❧

**calorie controlled cooking
spray**

300 g (10½ oz) leeks, sliced

**300 g (10½ oz) carrots, peeled
and cut into 1 cm (½ inch)
dice**

**250 g (9 oz) mushrooms,
sliced**

**250 g (9 oz) Savoy cabbage,
shredded**

**2 cm (¾ inch) fresh root
ginger, chopped finely**

**300 g (10½ oz) low fat soft
cheese**

**150 g (5½ oz) low fat natural
yogurt**

2 eggs, beaten

**350 g (12 oz) filo pastry,
defrosted if frozen**

**salt and freshly ground black
pepper**

*An exceptionally beautiful and tasty pie fit for a celebratory
meal.*

1 Preheat the oven to Gas Mark 4/180°C/fan oven 160°C. Heat
a large saucepan and spray with the cooking spray. Add the
leeks and carrots and stir fry for 5 minutes. Add the mushrooms,
cabbage and ginger and cook for a further 2 minutes.

2 Tip the vegetable mixture into a bowl and allow it to cool. In
another bowl, whisk the soft cheese, yogurt and eggs together.
Season and pour this over the vegetables.

3 Spray the inside of a 20 cm (8 inch) springform cake tin with
the cooking spray and line with a few of the filo pastry sheets.
Spray the pastry with the cooking spray and then add more
sheets, overlapping them to line the base and sides of the tin
so that there are no gaps (the sheets will hang over the edge
of the tin).

4 Spoon the vegetable mixture into the tin. Fold in the filo pastry
that is hanging over the edges of the tin so that it covers the
vegetables. Spray the remaining sheets of filo pastry with the
cooking spray and cut into 2.5 cm (1 inch) strips.

5 Cover the surface of the pie with the strips, arranging them
decoratively, and then spray again. Bake for 35–40 minutes until
golden brown and crisp all over. Allow to stand for 5 minutes to
cool a little. Remove from the tin and serve.

B'stilla roll

Serves 4

273 calories per serving

Takes 20 minutes to prepare
+ 10 minutes cooling,
45 minutes to cook

Ⓥ

4 eggs

½ x 25 g packet fresh flat leaf
parsley, chopped roughly

½ x 25 g packet fresh
coriander, chopped roughly

1 preserved lemon from a jar,
drained, pips removed and
diced finely

350 g packet Quorn Chicken
Style Pieces

a generous pinch of saffron

1 tablespoon cornflour

8 x 15 g (½ oz) filo pastry
sheets, measuring
30 x 40 cm (12 x 16 inches)

calorie controlled cooking
spray

15 g (½ oz) flaked almonds

freshly ground black pepper

*This adaptation of the Moroccan b'stilla pie is great hot
or cold. Serve with a generous mixed salad, gherkins and
pickled onions.*

1 Preheat the oven to Gas Mark 4/180°C/fan oven 160°C. Put
3 eggs into a small saucepan, cover with water and bring to the
boil. Simmer for 8 minutes, drain and plunge into cold water.

2 Meanwhile, in a large bowl, mix together the parsley,
coriander, diced lemon, Quorn pieces, saffron and freshly
ground black pepper. Dissolve the cornflour in 2 tablespoons
of cold water to make a paste. Peel the eggs and chop roughly.
Stir into the Quorn mixture with the cornflour paste.

3 Lay a sheet of filo pastry on a non stick baking tray and
spray with the cooking spray. Take a second filo sheet and lay
it next to the first, overlapping one long edge slightly to make
a rectangle measuring 30 x 25 cm (12 x 10 inches). Spray
again with the cooking spray and repeat the layering until all
the sheets are used.

4 Spread the Quorn mixture over the rectangle leaving a
2.5 cm (1 inch) border all the way around. Spray the exposed
filo pastry with the cooking spray and fold over the pastry of
the two short sides. Roll up the pastry starting from one long
side like a big Swiss roll.

5 Beat the remaining egg and brush over the pastry. Sprinkle
with the almonds and bake for 40–45 minutes. Leave to cool
for 10 minutes, cut into four and serve immediately.

Variation... For a tasty chicken version, see page 103.

Colourful couscous casserole

Serves 6

272 calories per serving

Takes 20 minutes to prepare,
40–45 minutes to cook

Ⓥ

250 g (9 oz) dried couscous
1 teaspoon olive oil
125 ml (4 fl oz) boiling water
2 large onions, chopped
125 ml (4 fl oz) hot vegetable
stock
3 or 4 garlic cloves, crushed
2 leeks, sliced
1 red pepper, de-seeded and
sliced
1 green pepper, de-seeded and
sliced
1 yellow pepper, de-seeded
and sliced
100 g (3½ oz) broccoli, broken
into florets
8 mushrooms, sliced
150 g (5½ oz) baby corn
2 x 400 g cans chopped
tomatoes
6 tomatoes, sliced
salt and freshly ground black
pepper
fresh parsley sprigs, to
garnish (optional)

*This is a brilliant dish for feeding friends, and it's suitable
for vegetarians and vegans too. Serve any leftovers cold as
a salad.*

1 Put the couscous into a large mixing bowl and add the olive oil
and boiling water, stirring to mix. Cover and leave for 5 minutes.
Preheat the oven to Gas Mark 3/170°C/fan oven 150°C.

2 Put the onions, stock and garlic into a large frying pan and
cook for 5 minutes.

3 Stir the onion mixture into the couscous with all the remaining
vegetables and the chopped tomatoes, but not the sliced fresh
tomatoes. Season well.

4 Transfer the couscous mixture to a large, lidded, ovenproof
dish and arrange the sliced tomatoes on top. Cover and bake
for 30–40 minutes.

5 Remove the lid, garnish with the parsley, if using, and serve.

Variations... For a fishy meal, top the couscous with a
grilled or baked 120 g (4¼ oz) cod steak per person and
garnish with watercress.

Vary the vegetables according to the season and your
own preferences.

Red pepper and basil cheesecake

Serves 6

194 calories per serving

Takes 35 minutes to prepare
+ 10 minutes cooling,
20 minutes to cook

Ⓥ

❄

For the pastry

**100 g (3½ oz) plain flour, plus
2 teaspoons for rolling**

1 tablespoon cornflour

50 g (1¾ oz) low fat spread

a pinch of salt

For the filling

**3 red peppers, de-seeded and
halved**

**350 g (12 oz) low fat plain
cottage cheese**

2 eggs

2 tablespoons torn fresh basil

**salt and freshly ground black
pepper**

*Not all cheesecakes have to be sweet, try this savoury
version and you'll be hooked.*

1 To make the pastry, mix the flour and cornflour together in
a bowl. Rub in the low fat spread with your fingertips until the
mixture resembles fine breadcrumbs. Add the salt and then stir
in enough cold water to make a soft dough.

2 Preheat the oven to Gas Mark 5/190°C/fan oven 170°C. On
a lightly floured surface, roll out the pastry so it is big enough
to line the base and sides of a 20 cm (8 inch) fluted loose
bottomed flan tin. Lift the pastry into the tin and prick the base
with a fork. Line with non stick baking parchment and baking
beans and bake blind for 10 minutes. Remove the beans and
the paper and return the pastry to the oven for 10 minutes.

3 Meanwhile, preheat the grill to high and grill the peppers,
skin side up, until the skins blacken and blister. Transfer the
peppers to a polythene bag and seal. When they are cool
enough to handle, peel off the skins and roughly chop the flesh.

4 Place the peppers, cottage cheese, eggs, basil and seasoning
in a food processor and blend until smooth. Remove the pastry
case from the oven and spoon in the pepper filling.

5 Return the flan to the oven for 20 minutes until the filling has
set and is firm to the touch. Allow to cool for 10 minutes before
slicing into wedges to serve.

Tip... If you don't have a food processor, chop the red
pepper very finely and push the cottage cheese through
a sieve. Mix them together with the eggs, basil and
seasoning as in step 5 before spooning into the case.

Party time

Sesame prawn toasts

Makes 12

75 calories per serving

Takes 25 minutes to prepare,
6–8 minutes to cook

80 g (3 oz) cooked peeled
   prawns, defrosted if frozen
80 g (3 oz) pork mince
1 spring onion, sliced finely
1 garlic clove, crushed
1 egg, beaten
½ teaspoon fish sauce
1 tablespoon chopped fresh
   coriander
150 g (5½ oz) French stick,
   cut into 1 cm (½ inch) thick
   slices
2 tablespoons sesame seeds
salt and freshly ground black
   pepper
2 tablespoons sweet chilli
   sauce, to serve

A healthier version of this popular starter.

1 Place the prawns in a blender and blend until nearly smooth. Add the pork and blend together with the prawns.

2 Place the prawn and pork mixture in a bowl and add the spring onion, garlic, egg, fish sauce and coriander. Season and mix well.

3 Heat a small non stick frying pan and cook the prawn mixture for 3–4 minutes, stirring constantly.

4 Preheat the grill to medium and toast the French stick slices on one side. Spoon the prawn mixture on to the untoasted side of the bread. Press down well and then sprinkle with the sesame seeds.

5 Grill for 3–4 minutes, until the sesame seeds start to turn golden. Serve with the chilli sauce.

Tip... When buying fresh coriander, choose deep green leaves – these will be the freshest and tastiest.

Smoked salmon and prawn bites

Makes 12 bites
29 calories per serving
Takes 10 minutes + chilling

50 g (1¾ oz) low fat plain cottage cheese

50 g (1¾ oz) low fat soft cheese

75 g (2¾ oz) cooked peeled prawns, defrosted if frozen, chopped roughly

1 teaspoon snipped fresh chives

grated zest of ½ a lemon

125 g (4½ oz) smoked salmon slices

freshly ground black pepper

These luxurious little party bites are a doddle to make but look really impressive. Chill well before slicing, to keep the shape.

1 Press the cottage cheese through a sieve into a bowl and then blend in the soft cheese. Stir in the prawns, chives, lemon zest and black pepper.

2 Lay two pieces of cling film out flat on your work surface and place two slices of smoked salmon on each, side by side and slightly overlapping. Spoon the prawn mixture down the centre and use the cling film to help you roll the smoked salmon around the filling, to enclose it.

3 Wrap the smoked salmon rolls up tightly in the cling film and twist the ends to secure. Chill in the fridge for at least 30 minutes to firm up. Cut each roll into six bites to serve and arrange on a plate.

Tip... See page 142 for the Marinated olives in this photo, and page 143 for the Creamy houmous with vegetable dippers.

Marinated olives

Serves 8

45 calories per serving

Takes 10 minutes +
marinating

Ⓥ

**400 g (14 oz) stoned black and
green olives in brine, drained**

1 teaspoon coriander seeds

1 teaspoon cumin seeds

**4 pared strips of rind and juice
from a lemon**

**4 pared strips of rind and juice
from an orange**

3 fresh thyme sprigs

2 garlic cloves, sliced

**a pinch of chilli flakes
(optional)**

*Prepare these olives a day ahead if you can, to get the
maximum flavour from the marinade.*

1 Place the olives on a chopping board and lightly crush
with a rolling pin, so that all the flavours of the marinade can
penetrate, then place in a bowl.

2 Toast the coriander and cumin seeds in a small frying pan
for 30 seconds or until they smell aromatic.

3 Add the citrus rinds and juices, thyme, garlic and chilli
flakes, if using, to the frying pan and warm through briefly.
Pour over the olives, cover and marinate in the fridge for at
least 4 hours, but preferably overnight.

Creamy houmous with vegetable dippers

Serves 8
141 calories per serving
Takes 20 minutes
🟢

2 x 410 g cans chick peas, drained and rinsed
300 g (10½ oz) 0% fat Greek yogurt
grated zest and juice of a lemon
2 garlic cloves, crushed
½ teaspoon ground cumin, plus a pinch to serve
salt and freshly ground black pepper

To serve
250 g (9 oz) cauliflower, broken into small florets
2 red peppers, de-seeded and sliced
2 yellow peppers, de-seeded and sliced
125 g (4½ oz) mange tout
4 carrots, peeled and cut into batons
285 g (10 oz) cherry tomatoes

Perfect for parties, this colourful platter of crudités and houmous also makes a great informal sharing starter with drinks before dinner.

1 Place the chick peas in a food processor with the yogurt, lemon zest and juice, garlic and cumin. Whizz to a purée, adding 6–8 tablespoons of water as needed to get the right consistency. Season to taste, spoon into a serving bowl and dust with a little extra ground cumin.

2 Arrange the vegetable dippers on a platter and serve with the houmous.

Glazed sausage kebabs

Makes 8 kebabs

189 calories per serving

Takes 10 minutes to prepare,
  15 minutes to cook

**450 g (1 lb) low fat pork
  sausages, each cut into
  three**

2 courgettes, sliced thickly

8 small tomatoes, halved

**2 dessert apples, cored,
  quartered and cut into
  eighths**

4 small onions, quartered

For the glaze

2 tablespoons mango chutney

2 tablespoons orange juice

**1 tablespoon wholegrain
  mustard**

½ teaspoon ground ginger

These make great party food for sharing.

1 To make the glaze, gently heat all the ingredients together in a small saucepan.

2 Heat the grill to medium. Thread the sausage pieces, courgettes, tomatoes, apples and onions alternatively on to eight small metal skewers.

3 Grill the kebabs for 12–15 minutes, turning and brushing them with the glaze. Mix any grill pan juices with any leftover glaze and dribble this over the kebabs.

Tip... If using wooden skewers, soak them in water for 30 minutes first to prevent them from catching fire.

Variation... Replace the apples with chunks of pineapple or apricot halves and use the natural juice from the cans instead of the orange juice in the glaze.

Baby potato bites

Makes 16 mini potato halves
31 calories per coronation chicken serving
27 calories per crème fraîche and chilli serving
Takes 15 minutes to prepare + cooling, 30–40 minutes to cook

8 x 40 g (1½ oz) potatoes (e.g. Charlotte)
2 tablespoons olive oil
coarse ground salt and black pepper

For the coronation chicken topping
25 g (1 oz) cooked skinless chicken breast,
  chopped
1 tablespoon chopped red pepper
2 tablespoons virtually fat free fromage frais
1 teaspoon curry paste
1 teaspoon mango chutney
chopped fresh parsley, to garnish

For the crème fraîche and chilli topping
2 tablespoons half fat crème fraîche
1 teaspoon finely chopped green chilli
1 spring onion, chopped finely

These little roasted potatoes with their tasty toppings will go down a treat with everyone.

1 Preheat the oven to Gas Mark 5/190°C/fan oven 170°C. Toss the potatoes in the oil and tip into a shallow roasting tin. Season and roast for 30–40 minutes until tender. Leave until cool enough to handle.

continues overleaf ▶

2 Meanwhile make up the toppings – each is sufficient for four potato halves. Simply combine the ingredients together for each option, leaving some chopped herbs to garnish.

3 Cut the potatoes in half and then top with your choice of topping(s). Arrange on a plate and serve immediately.

Tip... The potatoes can be cooked up to 2 hours ahead. Do not cut them in half until needed. Cool, cover and keep in the refrigerator. Either warm up before serving or serve them at room temperature.

Variations... For the extra potato halves, try a blue cheese and chive topping. Mix together 25 g (1 oz) of blue cheese, 1 tablespoon of half fat crème fraîche and 1 teaspoon of chopped chives.

For a prawn and tomato salsa topping, mix together 2 tablespoons of 95% fat free tomato salsa, 8 cooked peeled prawns (defrosted if frozen) and 4 tiny fresh coriander sprigs.

Filo parcels

Makes about 30

35 calories per serving

Takes 35 minutes to prepare,
15 minutes to cook

Ⓥ

2 tablespoons currants

50 g (1¾ oz) pine nut kernels

1 tablespoon cumin seeds

175 g (6 oz) carrots, peeled
and grated coarsely

1 tablespoon ground
cinnamon

2 tablespoons chopped fresh
parsley or coriander

calorie controlled cooking
spray

1 onion, chopped finely

2 garlic cloves, chopped finely

10 x 15 g (½ oz) filo pastry
sheets, measuring
30 x 40 cm (12 x 16 inches),
defrosted if frozen

salt and freshly ground black
pepper

*These little Greek pies can be stuffed with any assortment
of tasty fillings.*

1 Place the currants in a small bowl, add 2 tablespoons of
water and soak for 10 minutes. Drain off any excess water.

2 Meanwhile, toast the pine nut kernels and cumin seeds in a
dry frying pan until golden brown. Mix them together in a bowl
with the currants, carrots, cinnamon and parsley or coriander
and season.

3 Heat a non stick frying pan, spray with the cooking spray
and fry the onion and garlic for 4 minutes, adding a splash of
water if they start to stick. Add to the other ingredients and mix
well. Preheat the oven to Gas Mark 4/180°C/fan oven 160°C
and spray two baking trays with the cooking spray.

4 Cut the filo pastry sheets into three lengthways. Keep them
covered with a damp tea towel until you are ready to use them.

5 For the next step, leave the sheets of filo pastry on the stack
while working with them. If you peel them off to work on them,
they will crumble and stick to the counter. Working with three
strips of pastry at a time, spray with the cooking spray and
place a heaped tablespoon of the filling on to the top right hand
corner of each strip. Fold down the corner to make a triangle
and continue to flip the filled triangle down the length of the filo
strip to wrap in the pastry. Place the filo triangles on a baking
sheet and spray with a little more cooking spray. Repeat to use
up all the filling.

6 Bake the parcels for 15 minutes until crisp and a deep
golden brown colour.

Vegetable and anchovy rolls

Makes 10

65 calories per serving

Takes 30 minutes to prepare
  + rising, 15 minutes to cook

145 g packet pizza dough mix

calorie controlled cooking spray

½ red pepper, de-seeded and diced

1 small red onion, diced

1 small courgette, diced

1 vine ripened tomato, chopped roughly

1 tablespoon fresh thyme leaves

a handful of fresh basil leaves

15 g (½ oz) canned anchovies in oil, drained, rinsed and chopped

1 tablespoon tomato purée

1 tablespoon plain flour, for dusting

You can vary the ingredients – try a little chilli, chopped ham or olives in brine.

1 Make up the pizza dough following the packet instructions and leave to rise for 10 minutes. Preheat the oven to Gas Mark 5/190°C/fan oven 170°C.

2 Spray a large non stick frying pan with the cooking spray and heat until hot. Add the pepper, onion and courgette and stir fry for 5 minutes, adding a splash of water if they start to stick. Add the tomato and thyme and cook for a further 5 minutes. Stir in the basil, anchovies and tomato purée. Set aside.

3 On a surface lightly dusted with flour, roll out the dough to a 30 x 20 cm (12 x 8 inch) rectangle. Spread over the vegetable mixture evenly. Roll up from one long side and slice into 10 rounds. Place on a baking tray lined with non stick baking parchment and bake for 15 minutes until golden.

Tip... These keep in an airtight container in the fridge for up to 3 days.

Falafels

Makes 20

49 calories per serving

Takes 20 minutes to prepare
+ overnight soaking
+ 50 minutes standing,
25 minutes to cook

Enjoy these satisfying Mediterranean patties with a 60 g (2 oz) warmed pitta bread and a green salad.

1 Place the chick peas in a bowl, cover with water and set aside to soak overnight in the fridge.

2 When ready to cook, rinse the bulgar wheat with cold water in a sieve. Place in a bowl, cover with the boiling water and leave to swell for 20 minutes.

3 Drain the chick peas and place in a blender with the bulgar wheat and all the other ingredients except the cooking spray. Whizz to a paste like consistency. Cover and leave to stand for 30 minutes.

4 Using wet hands, shape tablespoons of the mixture into 20 thin patties, about 4 cm (1½ inches) in diameter.

5 Spray a large non stick frying pan with the cooking spray and fry the patties in batches for 3 minutes on each side. To check that they are cooked through, break one in half; the colour should be even all the way through to the middle. If not, increase the cooking time by a minute.

225 g (8 oz) dried chick peas

75 g (2¾ oz) dried bulgar wheat

700 ml (1¼ pints) boiling water

1 garlic clove

4 spring onions, chopped finely

3 tablespoons fresh flat leaf parsley, chopped

1 teaspoon ground coriander

1 teaspoon ground cumin

¼ teaspoon cayenne pepper

1 tablespoon lemon juice

½ teaspoon bicarbonate of soda

calorie controlled cooking spray

salt and freshly ground black pepper

Desserts and bakes

Baked poppy seed and lemon cheesecake

Serves 8

282 calories per serving

Takes 20 minutes to prepare
+ 1 hour chilling,
30–40 minutes to bake

Ⓥ

125 g (4½ oz) light digestive biscuits, crushed

25 g (1 oz) low fat spread, melted

150 g (5½ oz) golden caster sugar

1 tablespoon cornflour, sifted

grated zest of 2 lemons

2 teaspoons vanilla extract

300 g (10½ oz) low fat soft cheese

200 g (7 oz) half fat crème fraîche

110 g (4 oz) 0% fat Greek yogurt

2 eggs, beaten

1 tablespoon poppy seeds

This recipe is based on the classic New York style baked cheesecake. It keeps well in the fridge for 2–3 days.

1 Preheat the oven to Gas Mark 6/200°C/fan oven 180°C. Line the base of a 20 cm (8 inch) springform cake tin with non stick baking parchment.

2 Combine the crushed biscuits with the melted low fat spread and 1 tablespoon of water. Press evenly into the base of the tin. Chill until required.

3 Place the sugar, cornflour and lemon zest in a food processor and blend briefly. Add the vanilla extract, soft cheese, crème fraîche, yogurt and eggs and blend until smooth.

4 Pour the mixture over the base and sprinkle with the poppy seeds. Bake for 30–40 minutes until the cheesecake has begun to shrink from the sides of the tin and is golden on top – it should still wobble slightly in the middle but will firm up on cooling. Leave to cool before removing from the tin and then chill for at least 1 hour. Don't worry if the cheesecake cracks.

Chocolate raspberry roulade

Serves 8

149 calories per serving

Takes 20 minutes to prepare,
    15 minutes to cook

♥

❄

4 eggs

110 g (4 oz) caster sugar

**50 g (1¾ oz) cocoa powder,
½ teaspoon reserved for
dusting**

**25 g (1 oz) roasted chopped
hazelnuts**

**200 g (7 oz) fat free fromage
frais**

½ teaspoon vanilla extract

15 g (½ oz) teaspoon honey

**80 g (3 oz) raspberries,
crushed roughly**

*This flour free roulade makes an attractive centrepiece for
a buffet table.*

1 Preheat the oven to Gas Mark 6/200°C/fan oven 180°C.
Line a 32 x 23 cm (13 x 9 inch) baking tin with non stick
baking parchment.

2 Place the eggs and sugar in a heatproof bowl over a pan of
simmering water. Using an electric whisk, beat until thick and
creamy; the whisks should leave a trail when lifted.

3 Remove from the heat and sift over the cocoa powder. Gently
fold in until combined. Pour into the prepared tin and level the
surface with the back of a spoon. Bake for 15 minutes until
springy in the middle.

4 Place a damp tea towel on a wire rack with a sheet of
greaseproof paper on top. Scatter over the hazelnuts. Tip the
cake out on to the nuts and carefully remove the paper it is
baked on. Trim the crusty edges and discard. Roll the roulade
up with the paper inside it and leave to cool completely. Don't
worry if it cracks.

5 Mix together the fromage frais, vanilla extract and honey
and then stir in the raspberries. Unroll the roulade and spread
over the fromage frais mixture. Roll it up again and dust with
the reserved cocoa to serve.

Tips... You can make this dessert up to 2 hours in advance
but keep the cocoa powder for dusting at the last minute.

If you wish, you can freeze the whole filled roulade,
reserving the cocoa powder for dusting just before serving;
simply defrost in the fridge overnight before serving.

Whole apple tarts

Serves 4

282 calories per serving

Takes 15 minutes to prepare
+ 10 minutes standing,
40 minutes to bake

*These individual puddings are so impressive and fuss free.
Serve with 1 tablespoon 0% fat Greek yogurt.*

1 Preheat the oven to Gas Mark 4/180°C/fan oven 160°C.
Put the low fat spread and sugar in a small saucepan and
gently heat until the sugar has dissolved. Bubble for 1 minute.

2 Divide the melted sugar between four 200 ml (7 fl oz)
ramekins. Using an apple corer, remove the core from each
apple and discard. Carefully slice a little from the bottom of
each apple so it stands flat. Put an apple into each ramekin,
with the flat bottom upwards.

3 Mix together the sultanas, ginger and lemon juice and use
to fill the centre of each apple. Unroll the pastry and lightly roll
to make it slightly larger. Cut the pastry into four circles, big
enough to just cover the top of each ramekin.

4 Cover each ramekin with a circle of pastry and brush the
tops with the milk. Bake in the oven for 40 minutes until golden.
Remove from the oven and leave to stand for 5–10 minutes.

5 To serve, carefully loosen the pastry from the sides of the
ramekin and upturn on to a plate. Remove the ramekins and
serve.

Tip... Make these up to 1 day in advance and chill in the
fridge until needed.

15 g (½ oz) low fat spread
**50 g (1¾ oz) light muscovado
sugar**
4 dessert apples
30 g (1¼ oz) golden sultanas
**15 g (½ oz) fresh root ginger,
grated**
juice of a lemon
**125 g (4½ oz) ready rolled puff
pastry**
1 tablespoon skimmed milk

Fruit brûlée

Serves 4
93 calories per serving
Takes 10 minutes +
  30 minutes chilling

125 g (4½ oz) blueberries
125 g (4½ oz) redcurrants
artificial sweetener (optional)
15 ml (½ fl oz) Drambuie or
  other liqueur
300 g (10½ oz) low fat set
  natural yogurt
4 heaped teaspoons demerara
  sugar

This is a quick but good looking sweet.

1 Divide the fruit between four ramekin dishes and sprinkle with artificial sweetener, if using. Pour over the liqueur and then spoon on the yogurt. Refrigerate for 30 minutes.

2 Preheat the grill to the highest setting. Top each ramekin with a heaped teaspoon of demerara sugar and grill for 1–2 minutes, until the sugar is bubbling and golden. Chill until ready to serve.

Lemon soufflés

Serves 4
71 calories per serving
Takes 30 minutes
Ⓥ

calorie controlled cooking
  spray
2 teaspoons caster sugar
grated zest of a lemon
3 tablespoons lemon curd
3 large egg whites

Soufflés are ideal for when you are entertaining as they always look so impressive.

1 Preheat the oven to Gas Mark 6/200°C/fan oven 180°C.

2 Spray four ramekin dishes with the cooking spray. Using 1 teaspoon of caster sugar, coat the dishes by shaking the sugar around one dish and then sprinkling the excess into the next one. Do this until the teaspoon of sugar is used.

3 In a small bowl, beat the lemon zest into the lemon curd.

4 In a clean, grease-free bowl, whisk the egg whites until stiff peaks form. Add the remaining caster sugar and whisk for 1 minute more. Fold the lemon curd mixture into the egg whites.

6 Spoon the soufflé mixture into the four ramekin dishes. Place them on a baking tray and cook in the oven for 10–12 minutes until the soufflés are risen and golden. Serve immediately.

Tip... Always make sure the bowl you are using to whisk egg whites is completely free of grease, or the egg whites will not whisk up.

Variations... This recipe also works well using orange curd and orange zest.

If you want to make the soufflés a little richer, place an additional ½ teaspoon of lemon curd in the bottom of each ramekin dish before adding the egg white mixture.

Pots au chocolat

Serves 6

153 calories per serving

Takes 25 minutes to prepare
+ 30 minutes chilling

60 g (2 oz) plain chocolate
(minimum 70% cocoa
solids), broken into pieces

2 teaspoons unsweetened
cocoa powder

1 tablespoon caster sugar

2 eggs, separated

100 ml (3½ fl oz) whipping
cream

*These little French chocolate pots are rich and delicious –
the perfect finale for a special meal.*

1 Put the chocolate into a small heavy based saucepan with
the cocoa powder, sugar and 4 tablespoons of hot water. Heat
gently, stirring the mixture constantly until melted and smooth.
Do not let the mixture get too hot.

2 Pour the chocolate mixture into a bowl. Add the egg yolks
and stir well. Cover the surface with a circle of dampened
greaseproof paper to prevent a skin from forming and set aside
to cool for about 15 minutes.

3 Whip the cream in a chilled bowl until it holds its shape and
then spoon half of it into the cooled chocolate mixture. Chill the
remaining cream.

4 In a clean, grease-free bowl, and using a very clean whisk
or electric beaters, whisk the egg whites until stiff peaks form.
Fold them gently into the chocolate mixture. Divide the mixture
between six small pots or serving glasses and chill for at least
30 minutes, or until ready to serve.

5 Just before serving, top each dessert with a spoonful of the
reserved cream to decorate.

Tip... Remember that this recipe contains raw eggs, so
it may not be suitable for the very old or young, or for
pregnant women.

Devil's food cake

Makes 10 slices
231 calories per serving
Takes 30 minutes to prepare +
   cooling, 25 minutes to bake
Ⓥ

**calorie controlled cooking
   spray**
100 g (3½ oz) low fat spread
**150 g (5½ oz) light brown soft
   sugar**
2 eggs
**40 g (1½ oz) plain chocolate
   (minimum 70% cocoa solids)**
100 ml (3½ fl oz) boiling water
150 g (5½ oz) plain flour
½ teaspoon baking powder
**1 teaspoon bicarbonate of
   soda**
**100 g (3½ oz) low fat natural
   yogurt**
1 teaspoon vanilla essence

For the filling
50 g (1¾ oz) low fat spread
**50 g (1¾ oz) icing sugar, plus
   extra for dusting**
**1 teaspoon cocoa powder, plus
   extra for dusting**

*This full-blown chocolate cake is temptation indeed. It's
for a special occasion when nothing but chocolate cake
will do, but it's a healthier version.*

1 Preheat the oven to Gas Mark 5/190°C/fan oven 170°C.
Spray two 18 cm (7 inch) cake tins with the cooking spray, line
the bases with non stick baking parchment and spray again.

2 Cream the low fat spread and brown sugar together until
light and fluffy. Add the eggs one at a time, beating well
between each addition.

3 Break up the chocolate into a saucepan, pour the boiling
water over and heat gently until smooth and thick. Cool a little
and then add to the creamed mixture and blend well.

4 Sift the flour with the baking powder and bicarbonate
of soda and add to the mixture with the yogurt and vanilla
essence. Mix well, pour into the prepared tins and bake for
25 minutes or until risen and a skewer inserted into the middle
comes out clean.

5 Turn out the cakes and leave on a wire rack to cool.
Meanwhile, make the filling by beating together the low fat
spread, icing sugar and cocoa powder until fluffy. Use to
sandwich together the cooled cakes. Dust the top with cocoa
powder or icing sugar and serve.

Marbled vanilla and coffee cake

Makes 12 slices
136 calories per serving
Takes 20 minutes to prepare,
35 minutes to bake

Ⓥ
❄

100 g (3½ oz) low fat spread
100 g (3½ oz) caster sugar
2 eggs
175 g (6 oz) self raising flour
3 tablespoons skimmed milk
1 teaspoon vanilla essence
3 tablespoons strong black coffee

For the topping
100 g (3½ oz) low fat soft cheese
1 teaspoon strong black coffee
2 tablespoons artificial sweetener

This is great fun to make. The best part is slicing into the cake and seeing the marbled patterns.

1 Preheat the oven to Gas Mark 5/190°C/fan oven 170°C. Line a 20 cm (8 inch) round cake tin with non stick baking parchment.

2 Cream the low fat spread and sugar together until the mixture is pale and fluffy. Add the eggs and beat well. Sift the flour into the mixture and fold it in thoroughly using a metal spoon.

3 Divide the mixture between two bowls. Mix the skimmed milk and vanilla essence into one bowl and the coffee into the other.

4 Drop alternating spoonfuls of the mixture into the prepared tin, dragging a skewer through the mixtures to blend them into each other. Bake for 30–35 minutes until the cake is well risen and springy to the touch.

5 Carefully remove the cake from the tin and allow it to cool completely on a wire rack.

6 To decorate, beat the soft cheese with the coffee and sweetener and spread it over the surface, using a fork to mark a pattern on the top.

Coconut and raspberry cup cakes

Makes 10

209 calories per serving

Takes 15 minutes to prepare,
15 minutes to bake

These golden cup cakes are very light and have a wonderful texture from the coconut and a lovely sharp flavour from the raspberries. Serve with more fresh raspberries and virtually fat free fromage frais for a dessert, or for tea with fruit or herb teas.

25 g (1 oz) ground almonds
50 g (1¾ oz) desiccated coconut
225 g (8 oz) icing sugar
50 g (1¾ oz) plain flour
½ teaspoon baking powder
125 g (4½ oz) low fat spread, melted
5 egg whites
100 g (3½ oz) raspberries, fresh or frozen

1 Preheat the oven to Gas Mark 4/180°C/fan oven 160°C. Place 10 cup cake cases in a Yorkshire pudding or muffin tin.

2 Mix the ground almonds, coconut, sugar, flour and baking powder together in a bowl. Add the melted low fat spread and mix to combine.

3 In a clean, grease-free bowl, whisk the egg whites until they form stiff peaks and then fold gently into the almond mixture.

4 Pour the mixture into the cup cake cases and sprinkle the raspberries over the top of each cake.

5 Bake for 12–15 minutes or until the cakes are golden and springy to the touch.

Sticky cinnamon buns

Makes 8 buns

82 calories per serving

Takes 25 minutes to prepare + cooling, 12 minutes to bake

Ⓥ
❄

110 g (4 oz) self raising flour, plus ½ tablespoon for rolling
½ teaspoon baking powder
1½ tablespoons low fat spread
finely grated zest of ½ a lemon
1 tablespoon skimmed milk
15 g (½ oz) light brown soft sugar
¾ teaspoon ground cinnamon
1 tablespoon golden syrup

This recipe is wonderfully indulgent.

1 Preheat the oven to Gas Mark 7/220°C/fan oven 200°C.

2 Sieve the flour and baking powder into a large mixing bowl. Add 1 tablespoon of the low fat spread and rub it into the flour using your fingertips. Stir in the lemon zest and then gradually mix in enough milk to form a soft dough.

3 Sprinkle some of the remaining flour on a sheet of non stick baking parchment and use the rest to flour a rolling pin. Lightly knead the dough and then roll it out on the baking parchment to a 18 x 14 cm (7 x 5½ inch) rectangle.

4 Spread the remaining low fat spread over the dough, leaving about 1 cm (½ inch) clear along one long side.

5 Mix the sugar and cinnamon together and sprinkle over the low fat spread-covered dough. Brush the clear section of the dough with a little water. Using the baking parchment to help, roll up the dough from the covered long side to the clear side. Using a very sharp knife, cut the dough into eight slices.

6 Lay a piece of non stick baking parchment on a baking tray and arrange the slices, with a cut side facing up, on the paper. Leave a space between each bun. Bake for 12 minutes until light golden brown.

7 While the buns are cooking, spoon the syrup into a small bowl and then microwave on high for 3–4 seconds. Remove the buns from the oven and leave for 2–3 minutes until cool enough to handle. Brush some of the warm syrup over the tops and sides of the buns and serve warm.

Index